*Single Father's Handbook*

# Single Father's Handbook

## A Guide for Separated and Divorced Fathers

by *RICHARD H. GATLEY*, Ph.D.
and *DAVID KOULACK*, Ph.D.

ANCHOR BOOKS
Anchor Press/Doubleday, Garden City, New York
1979

The Anchor Books edition is the first publication of SINGLE FATHER'S HANDBOOK
Anchor Books edition: 1979

ISBN: 0-385-13653-6
Library of Congress Catalog Card Number 78-1204

*To Joshua, Daniel, Robert and Samantha*

# Contents

# Introduction

"My dad and mom don't live together," Robbie hollered to his friend, explaining why they couldn't play together after school. "They're separated."

"You sure had to tell him everything," his father complained.

"No, I didn't," he replied. "I didn't tell him how you used to fight."

"I guess you didn't, did you. Well we don't fight any more, do we, son?"

"Nope." He skipped ahead to the waiting car.

Dick's seven-year-old son seemed to accept the separation that simply. His four-year-old daughter gave it even less thought, but for us, it's been a bit more complicated and difficult. We even had to write a book about it.

We were standing in David's kitchen when we decided to write a book for people like ourselves—for separated fathers. As we washed dishes and made coffee, we talked about our recent experiences with our children, as we had talked many times before.

Over the years, we had come to the realization that fathers who are separated from their children have many problems in common even though the individuals, the circumstances of separation, and the ages of the children might be quite different. We found that sharing these experiences with each other and with other separated fathers who were friends or clients had often been instructive and helpful and sometimes had really gotten us out of some difficult situations.

It was helpful to know how other people had solved problems that we encountered, like how to entertain your kids on a rainy day, or how to tell them that your woman friend is moving in. Sometimes, it helped just to know that other separated fathers were experiencing similar difficulties, such as trying to make every visit with their children the "perfect" visit or having bouts of guilt about "abandoning" their children.

Because of this, we decided to write a book that shared with other separated fathers some of the things we've learned from our own experiences, and those of our clients and friends, and from our children. We've tried to provide some practical solutions to problems that separated fathers often encounter. But even more, we wanted to reassure the newly separated father that seemingly devastating events that arise in the process of separation, which seem to make continued fathering impossible, aren't really so unique and, more important, are not insurmountable.

While we don't expect to answer everyone's questions—or for this book to serve as an unfailing guide—we do hope you'll be able to pick it up in the midst of your worst "catastrophizing" and find the kind of good company, validation, and encouragement we found in each other.

We'd like to thank some of those who helped make this book possible. Immodestly enough, we offer first recognition to our own collaboration and to the "third author" who mercifully emerged out of the collision of our two very different writing styles. Were we glad to see him!

We're grateful, of course, to our children for still being our kids when the dust had settled, and to their mothers who also continue to share their love.

To our women friends, who loved and supported us in spite of our catastrophizing, we owe an additional debt of appreciation. They taught us some of the things we needed to know about women.

We feel kinship with those other separated fathers and mothers, friends and clients both, who shared their experiences, problems, and advice with us. This is their book as well as ours. We'd also like to thank the friends, relatives, and colleagues who encouraged and supported us, and our editors at Anchor/Doubleday who saw in our first short submission something worth printing.

Finally, we'd like to express our appreciation to you for being interested enough to pick up a book about separated fathers. We had you in mind as we wrote and we hope you'll like what we have to say.

David Koulack
Richard H. Gatley
Spring, 1979

# Who This Book Is For

When we talk about "separated fathers" we have in mind people rather like ourselves, naturally. The separated fathers we know are men who are separated from their children consequent to a separation from the mother of their children. It doesn't matter whether this separation comes about through divorce, legal separation, or by the parents simply not living with each other any more. But, although we'll discuss other and better arrangements, we do assume that the mother has "custody" of the children. They live with her, and their father has "visiting rights" which permit him to see the children at reasonably frequent intervals. We also assume that the separation, whether amicable or acrimonious, is experienced as permanent rather than as a brief trial.

"Our" separated fathers are relatively inexperienced, or at least out of practice, when it comes to living alone. Having depended a good deal on their ex-wives, they have little practical knowledge about taking care of themselves or their children. Nor do they have huge amounts of money to invest in hiring people to relieve them of their new responsibilities. We won't even count on the separated father having a woman friend willing to take on all of his ex-wife's former duties.

But perhaps the most basic and important assumption we make is that the separated father loves and wants his children. He might not look like it at first, as absorbed as he may be with separation from his wife. And he needn't feel himself particularly loving or even miss his children very much to begin with. But, once freed by the separation to nurture his kids in his own way, the separated father often becomes intensely involved with his children, surprising both himself and the outside observer when he takes up child-rearing tasks with unbridled enthusiasm and determination. So, despite the emotional storms of separation or divorce which may temporarily blind them, these are men who really care about their kids.

As far as the children themselves are concerned, we probably talk most knowledgeably about the problems that separated fathers might have in dealing with boys and girls from two to fifteen, the ages of our children over the course of our separations—problems ranging from changing diapers to keeping your nose out of your teen-ager's business. The varied experiences of our friends and clients who are separated have helped us fill in the gaps.

At the risk of sounding silly, we should mention that the separated fathers we feel qualified to talk about are males. We know women who are in the same boat as separated fathers, who don't have custody of their children, and who, because they may not want to be or weren't trained to be "mothers," experience many problems in common with the men we are talking about. We can't expect to speak for women in this fix, but we do hope these separated mothers will find our book sympathetic and helpful and that they will forgive us our masculine pronouns.

Our hope then is that both fathers and mothers who are separated from their children will find in this book some comfort, encouragement, and practical suggestions that will be useful for handling the many problems that come with separation from their children. We also hope that men and women who have already mastered most of the skills and who have already jumped some of the emotional hurdles we mention will recognize these familiar experiences along with us and in so doing find validation for themselves both as parents and as persons.

We have had others in mind throughout the writing of this book as well as separated fathers. In addition to enjoying the funny parts about themselves and us, we hope our kids will like it as a statement of our liking and love for them. We hope your children will share some of these things with our kids.

We earnestly hope mothers will read this book, because we believe it offers hope for and new perspectives on jointly caring for the children. We know how often women tend to write off their former husbands as uninterested, incompetent, or undeserving, often from painful experience. But separation itself can be a force and occasion for change of a creative and positive nature. It is urgent that both parents be able to perceive these possibilities. Actually, preliminary indications already suggest that a lot of separated fathers will probably receive their copy of this book as a gift and gentle hint from their former spouses.

Women who enter the lives of separated fathers find theirs a particularly difficult and often confusing path to follow. Through open discussion of the vulnerable and uncertain position of the "new woman" friend we hope to support their chances of finding satisfying lives with separated men who happen to have children.

Parents and friends of separated people may find clues in these pages to help them understand what is happening, permitting them to support both the separating family and the newly formed single-parent families. Much more can be done by people who are aware of the complications which these families face.

The same can certainly be said for educators, employers, and the professionals who come in contact with any and all of the people involved in this book. Schools can recognize and encourage the participation of separated fathers in the social and educational aspects of the lives of their children. Employers and colleagues can likewise appreciate the demands of separate fathering for time and energy, allowing men more of an opportunity to do a good job of fathering.

We firmly believe that professionals who are involved with any facet of the lives of separating families should find this book helpful. Lawyers and judges, most frequently in the middle of these things, we hope will understand our strong statements about the problems and inadequacies of the adversary system. We are aware that it is often a lawyer who plays the much-needed "Dutch uncle."

But this book emphasizes relationship rather than legal problems and solutions. It should be of special value to the various helping professions who work with separating families, whether they operate from social agencies, churches, consulting rooms, or even behind the neighborhood bar. We believe it offers a useful and much-needed reappraisal of the importance of the separated father to the welfare of his children as well as illustrating additional ways in which practitioners can be helpful to families in trouble.

Most of all, whether or not anyone else catches on to what we are trying to say here, this book is for us—separated fathers. We need to stand up for ourselves and to reaffirm our importance as parents.

# 1. Becoming a Separated Father

## Separation and Divorce as Foreground

At first it is separation itself that is foreground for the separated father. Fatherhood lies hidden in the background behind all of the personal drama involved in the process of parting.

Thoughts of the children arise, of course, but seldom with the immediacy or preoccupation that surrounds the father's concerns about his dissolving marriage. Kids tend to be bit players upstaged by the larger roles played by both parents. They may be seen only as objects of parental duty, as problems to solve, as sources of guilt, and for some, as impediments to deliverance from the marriage.

Children often lend themselves as scapegoats or pawns to the conflict between their parents. But even when they are not merely blurs or bullets and the process of separation is amicable, children, especially the younger ones, seldom come into their own right as persons until after the separation is completed.

We aren't saying that separated fathers don't care about their kids. But we are saying that it's very difficult for anyone caught up in the dissolution of a marriage to be able to attend fully to anyone else, however much they love them. And on the whole, we don't think that children are surprised if their separating parents are more absorbed with their own discomfort than with their children's. Because their fate is so closely tied to that of their parents, kids are probably more likely to be concerned with their parents' plight than with their own needs.

Most of us can recall, for instance, the incredible anxiety occasioned by fights between our parents when we were young. Battles between these two titans would scare the hell out of us, because at times we weren't sure what would happen to them, or to us. If we were crazy enough to make personal demands of them in the middle of one of those fights it was more likely heroically designed to distract them than actually to win full attention for ourselves. At least that's the way we remember it.

In drawing attention to the separating father's natural absorption with his own immediate experiences and needs, we wish to acknowledge and validate this reality as well as point out its potentially unfortunate consequences for fathering. We know that recollection of these events can be extremely painful and that it is easy for fathers to slip into feelings of guilt and remorse ruminating about this process in retrospect. We also know that guilt is more disabling than it is helpful. For this reason it's important for fathers to have a more complete and compassionate understanding of what has happened to them and to their families so they may develop the perspective they need to resume fathering after separation. Perhaps the best place to begin is by examining the process of separation itself.

## Preparation or Prelude to Separation

It might seem strange to talk about preparation for separation, as though people went about it knowing what they were doing. We don't think most people are aware of their preparations. But the fact is that separations don't just happen, even though it may appear that way to outsiders or to the participants themselves.

Before they split, most people go through extended periods of preparation for the event whether they are aware of doing so or not. The preparation may take weeks, months, or even years, the length of time depending on a lot of things including the extent of the couple's involvement with one another emotionally, physically, and materially. But perhaps most importantly it depends on their ability to recognize and articulate the fact that problems exist which call into question the continuance of their marriage.

## Avoiding the Problem

Many people deny that serious problems exist for their marriage precisely because they are afraid that bringing the issues into the open will lead to divorce. They feel that this potential catastrophe must be averted at all costs. Furthermore, acknowledgment of problem areas would almost certainly bring about unwanted confrontations and unpleasantness without any compensating assurance of resolution; not a very happy prospect. It may be a lot easier, therefore, to ignore low-level conflicts that exist in the futile hope that the difficulty rather than the marriage will magically go away.

Even when problems are finally acknowledged, indecisiveness may reign for a long time, the pluses and minuses of the marriage constantly shifting back and forth keeping the conflicts in balance. The sheer inertia of the marriage, the glue, the many strings that are attached to marriage make it very resistant to coming apart even after it is recognized that the relationship has been fatally damaged.

Because marriages, even "failing" ones, have usually served important needs for both parties, when a rift appears serious enough to end it, the love and caring previously submerged by the couple's differences may re-emerge to remind them that they will lose someone valued and important if they split. For some, the subsequent process of mourning the loss of a loved partner may actually delay open acceptance of both the seriousness of the problems and the ultimate possibility of separation. For couples with children, the potential dangers of separation are likely to appear greater and may generate even stronger efforts to deny the seriousness of difficulties or to maintain the marriage in spite of them.

## Consequences of Avoidance

For these and other reasons, couples with problems tend to behave very foolishly, hiding the difficulties from themselves and from each other while simultaneously escalating the unacknowledged conflicts. As a result, preparation for separation often takes the form of fights, which increase in frequency, intensity, and duration, and/or the development of a constant state of tension when the couple is together, which then leads to subtle ways of avoiding one another to reduce the tension. One or both partners may also begin to develop interests outside the family, sexually, socially, or vocationally, thus moving away from the family toward other sources of satisfaction.

All of these things are signs of trouble. They are ways of saying there is something very wrong with the marriage. And some people read it that way, concluding from these indications that they no longer want to live with one another. Friction and unpleasantness combined with obvious attempts to withdraw from one another may be sufficient to override or temporarily obscure the good facets in the relationship, preparing the way for separation.

But many partners do such a great job of blocking out these signs that they aren't prepared at all for the separation when it occurs. They seem willfully blind to all of the indications of trouble or to the seriousness of their predicament. More than one husband or wife has been dumped on the marriage counselor's steps in shocked disbelief.

Yet somebody must have been prepared for the split, or aware of its imminence at some level. Husbands or wives who establish extramarital liaisons may actually be preparing replacements ahead of time. Wives who begin to equip themselves with employable skills or other financial resources and husbands who begin to take an interest in the workings of a household may be getting ready for the big day.

Covert maneuvers of this kind may be helpful in preparing for separation, sparing the couple full realization of what they are doing while enabling them to move toward parting. It may also spare one of them the feeling of being responsible for the break if the other partner cracks first. But the fact that these maneuvers are not out front, where everyone knows what is going on, can also be destructive of more than just the marital relationship.

## Impact on the Children

As rough as the process is for the childless couple, it's even worse, as the cliché goes, when children are involved. If the prelude to separation takes the form of escalating battles and constant tension it will be unpleasant and frightening for the children. The behavior of the "preparing" couple's friends might help to illustrate the point.

Friends suddenly begin to avoid couples in trouble, often because they can't bear the tension or hostility. And if these people who can escape to the relative safety of their own homes can't stand being around you for a few hours, consider what it must be like for the kids, stuck in the same house with the two of you, watching the two most important people in the world ream each other.

In addition to having to observe and share in the pain of their parents, children are also sometimes willing to accept responsibility for the anger and hostility flying around the household, a responsibility which their parents may be happy to avoid. Working in clinics, we've seen kids do some pretty far-out things over the years, trying to take the heat off their parents by running away, getting into trouble at school, and so on. Clinic case loads are full of kids referred for all kinds of "behavioral problems" or other symptoms that often turn out to be stand-ins for parents in trouble with one another.

Some kids may even feel directly responsible for the strife, thinking they have somehow caused the growing rift between their parents. If a child is left with this belief, when the separation actually comes he may feel that he has driven one of his parents from the home. Subsequent confusion and guilt would make it easy for him to feel not only abandoned but justifiably so.

This is but one among many miserable scenarios we might imagine given the conditions described. But before we examine ways of circumventing or undoing these traumas, we'd like to mention a less dramatic, but nonetheless very important consequence of some of the more avoidant means often adopted for dealing with a failing marriage.

## Some Consequences for Fathering

Because the underlying focus is usually on the marital relationship rather than on the family, fathers who cope with problems in their marriage by turning to people and pursuits outside the family seldom realize that in the process of doing so *they have already begun to separate themselves from their children as well as from their wives*. The babies go out with the bath water, so to speak.

It is true that many families may stabilize at this point, establishing a kind of equilibrium based on avoidance and substitution which may prevent the marriage from breaking up. But fathering goes by the boards along with marital companionship in such cases, often without anyone being the wiser except perhaps the children. It is in cases like this that children and their fathers may actually benefit when a renewal of fathering is made possible by the final breakdown of the marriage.

## What Can You Do?

If all these dismal things are true, you may well ask how *does* one go about preparing for the big moment? In all probability the answer is simple—*inadequately*. No one is likely to be expert at separating, even with the best advice. Most people reading this book will probably already have made an incredible mess of things. Even if you haven't, there is probably nothing anyone can tell you to make separation a moment of ecstasy for you, your wife, or your children. Besides, most of us are too pigheaded to listen to good advice anyway.

Even so, we know that people can go about separating a lot better than they generally do, and that some of the more common mistakes that separated fathers make are either avoidable or recoverable later on. If you have made most of your messes already, there are still ways of going about repairing the damage, clearing the way for happier and more effective fathering after the separation. We know, for example, that even after-the-fact descriptions of the process are helpful to people. Most of us have gone through the separation process without understanding much of what was happening. We've acted a lot of the time under far too much emotional stress to be able to comprehend the purpose or impact of our own or others' actions. And our "explanations" for these events often have been more self-destructive than necessary. Recognition of our own behavior in descriptions of what other people have gone through may bring us much-needed understanding of ourselves and help us to make better sense of our own experiences.

Some comprehension of what we've come through may also free us from persisting in our mistakes, giving us an opportunity for more constructive action. So, you may find something of value in what follows even if it's "too late" for you.

However, if you are still in the middle of the separation process, catching on to even a few things may allow you to forestall some of the messes or mistakes before they've gone too far. It won't eliminate all of the pain or grief, but being aware of some of the pitfalls as well as some of the resources available to you to deal with them may help you to avoid a lot of unnecessary anguish.

## Some Possibilities

If you are only just at the point where you are beginning to worry about your marriage, we think one of the first things to do is to acknowledge that your relationship is in trouble. As soon as you are aware that there is even a remote possibility of your marriage heading toward separation or divorce, verbalize it. And then discuss it as soberly as you can. Complacent reliance on marital bonds to hold you together or to pull you through a crisis may reduce the seriousness with which you take these revelations about your marriage even when you're making them yourself, and may prevent you from bringing your full attention to bear on the issues. This is unfortunate because the changes threatening your marriage may not only be powerful, they may also be healthy, developmental ones nurtured and made possible by your marriage.

Many "failed" marriages have actually been successes in that they have provided the necessary support for the personal development of one or both partners. It may be very sad when developmental gains outstrip or outmode a relationship or the present form of the relationship, but it's even sadder if the healthy aspects are unappreciated, or if their force is underestimated. We all recognize the necessary and healthy aspects of other developmental stages in life, even when they are awkward and uncomfortable, like adolescence, but we know far too little about adult development. More often we are frightened by change and hide when we might better be curious and respectful of such important events. Yet if two people have come as far as they can together, might it not be better for them to part with some appreciation for each other than to continue to invalidate each other instead in a relationship they've outgrown?

The idea that healthy developmental forces may be involved in marital discord is but one of many possible constructions that can be introduced to people bumping heads in a marriage, presenting the couple broader possibilities for constructive ways of responding to their troubles with each other.

## Get Some Help

Many marriage counselors, therapists, and other practitioners who work with couples and families can be helpful to people in trouble because they have some understanding of the positive as well as the negative aspects of marital disharmony. A third party, unencumbered by prejudice, can bring fresh perspective and encouragement to your discussions, which may help you to sort out your problems together. You need someone both of you can listen to in good faith. But before you decide to work with that person, remember to assess the counselor's readiness to listen to you as well. In our view a marriage counselor ideally should be prepared to serve as a separation and divorce counselor if needed, as ready to help you part as he is to help you stay together. Any strong personal investment in making your marriage work may blunt the counselor's usefulness, cutting off validation and support when you most need it. Whatever the final outcome may be, it should be determined by the wishes of the individuals involved and not by the therapist.

The potential usefulness of any counselor, however, outweighs the risk of bias. On the whole, we can't say the same about lawyers. We heartily recommend you stay clear of them, certainly during the exploratory phase, because most lawyers are geared for divorce; that's their business. We also have reservations about using lawyers even when you have definitely decided on separation and divorce, but we'll talk about that later.

## Let Others Know

Whether you tell anyone else what you're doing, like parents, relatives, or friends, depends on how constructive or supportive you think they are likely to be. The more support you have from the community the better, because you won't be functioning very well, at work or socially. It is generally better if people know so that they can make allowances for you without treating you like you're sick or crazy. If the news is leaked to them through gossip, so much the better in some cases. It may permit some of your acquaintances to be supportive without also being intrusive. The community of people with marital troubles or who are otherwise sympathetic is also very large. So while you may desperately want privacy, secrecy is seldom necessary or desirable.

Of course, some people may want to share their own limited conceptions of marriage and divorce as well as their support. Don't be afraid to trust your own reactions to their advice. If it doesn't feel right to you, skip it, if it does, explore it further. But remember, while others may be genuinely sympathetic, they may not be entirely on the right track themselves. It's nice to be able to turn to someone, but we are all fellow seekers as it were. You'll have to feel your own way among the many paths and models offered you, with faith, we hope, in your own capacity to choose wisely.

## Particularly Your Children

Your kids are one set of people you don't want to keep guessing. When you know that your marriage is in trouble, let them know about it. Don't keep it a "secret." If the troubles you have been having are messy and the potential for separation great, they undoubtedly know that something is happening already. We suggest you confirm for them that you and their mother are having problems with each other. It may help them to understand what has been going on with you. Maintaining credibility with your children at this time may also be very important for their faith in you later.

You needn't go into gruesome detail in your discussions with the children. You should also be careful to avoid using the kids as judges, referees, or consultants. The point is to let them off the hook, not to involve them further. Emphasize that the problems are between you and their mother and haven't anything to do with what they've done. And tell them that you will keep them posted.

Obviously it will be difficult to speak to your children about it if they are very young, but it's worth a try even if they are only a bit verbal. Doing so may provide a foundation for understanding when they are older.

## The Separation

At some point you and your wife will either be relatively certain you want to remain in the relationship or one or both of you will be certain that you want out. If you are in the first category, great, you can stop reading here unless you want to find out what you missed. But if you're in the latter category, now's when all the fun begins.

Whether it's a graceful process of mutual agreement or a one-sided hysterical exit, the reality of separation is usually something of a jolt. The moment of full realization that you are separated, that you no longer "have to" be together, or no longer have the "right" to be together is a shock. And both parties, depending on the extent of their preparation, will be in this state of shock for some time throughout the process of separation.

A sense of disbelief and a feeling of unreality separates each of them not only from one another but from the rest of the world for a time. Perception is limited, with a sharp focus on personal needs for survival, especially for the one out in the cold. A preoccupation with the seemingly insurmountable emotional and practical problems may further numb or narrow thinking processes. And a sense of catastrophic loss may vie with a feeling of release from the long conflict.

In other words, at a time when important decisions will be made which will set the pattern for future interactions, neither of you will be firing on all cylinders. With a narrowed perspective, you won't be able to foresee things that will matter to you later. And your heightened feelings of the moment will be poor servants for your future interests. You wouldn't hire anyone in your condition even to fix your sink, yet you might try to handle this terribly important transaction by yourselves.

We suggest you get some help. The decisions involved are even more important life decisions than buying a car or a new house. So take time and care in going about it. One expert's rule of thumb is to spend at least as much time getting out of your marriage as you spent getting into it. Separation deserves at least as much time and respect as getting married, and more when you have children.

So let a third party help you let go of each other. A therapist, counselor, or religious adviser can not only help you see your parting in more positive ways, but may also be able to help you work out a mutually satisfactory separation or divorce agreement, including how you can best share in taking care of the kids. Very importantly, a counselor may be able to prepare you for the unexpected and often difficult task of working out some kind of co-operative relationship which will permit you to continue functioning as parents to your children.

We know when children are involved that a relationship of some kind between the separating parents will remain after divorce. We also know that most people with kids don't realize beforehand just how much of a relationship will actually be necessary after they've dissolved their marriage. The basis for co-operation and mutual respect that will be needed later on when this shocking fact becomes clear needs to get its start now, even if it didn't exist during the marriage. A counselor or therapist aware of what things are like afterward may be essential to this important change of stance, and can offer a safe and constructive place for the separated couple to work out later disputes or conflicts that are likely to arise in the process. This is certainly a better alternative than lawyers.

Lawyers are still a distinct liability at this time. Focusing on the individual client, lawyers tend to frame their work in terms of doing their best for the client within the adversary system prevalent in North America. The needs of the client for a co-operative relationship with the mother or father of their children after divorce, or the client's personal preference to be a good person rather than a "winner," are frequently overridden by their enthusiastic advocates, creating unwanted problems for clients and family alike.

The point of all this is not to castigate lawyers for doing their identified jobs well, nor to criticize the obvious inadequacies of the legal system, but rather to caution the buyer to beware. If you don't know what is in the best interests of you and your family, consult a marriage counselor or similar professional who can help you to make the right decisions. Don't go to the shoe store to buy your groceries.

## Plans for the Children

Some of the most important of the series of decisions separating parents have to make relate to the way in which they'll share responsibility for raising the children after they've separated. Whether it is clearly and carefully articulated or not, some plan will definitely come out of the process of separation. So if you don't want to be stuck with something completely unacceptable to you later, do some work on it beforehand if you can.

Before you adopt any particular plan, however, we'd like to draw your attention to a few important things. If you have slipped out of your relationship with your wife without noticing that the kids are still with her, *notice now*. As we mentioned previously, most people are so preoccupied with the breakdown of the marriage that they fail to realize that it is a family and not just a couple that is coming apart; the kids tend to get lost in the shuffle and decisions about who will care for them are often made by default without the slightest realization of what that will really mean after the separation. As a result, a lot of fathers belatedly realize they've given up the kids without ever having intended to do so.

Granted, many fathers may realize they are leaving the kids behind and think that's the way they want it. But these same individuals often discover they are very different men once they are out of the marriage, with different ways of looking at things afterward, particularly their relationship with their children.

One nurturant guy we know, for instance, who had been doing almost all of the "mothering" the last two years of his marriage was so fed up taking care of the kids by himself that he was willing to see them go off with his not-very-interested-in-mothering wife, completely forgetting how much he would be wanting his kids after he got some rest. We encouraged him to see beyond the immediate relief of shedding what had momentarily become an intolerable burden. It was fairly easy getting him to recall the goodies he got from fathering, putting him in touch again with his own need to be with his children. He also saw how much his kids needed him. Dropping his original assumption that his wife would "naturally" take the kids with her when she left, he again felt the joy of being with his children, and made plans to be with them after the divorce.

Fathers who think it's fine to leave the kids behind, because men aren't "supposed" to take care of their kids or because it never occurred to them to do so, often have a change of heart after the separation. Some who even went as far as identifying the children as a cause of their misery during the marriage and who were glad to be rid of them, frequently experience a change once they have "escaped." There's no real way of knowing how you'll feel when you're out. And burning your paternal bridges behind you can be a source of real and lasting pain later on. It may be wise, therefore, to take some precautions to prevent irrevocable losses.

## Precautions

If you are still in reasonably good communication with your wife, you may be able to make arrangements with her that are flexible, geared to changing circumstances and to your individual needs and those of your children. The agreement can be an organic one that can grow with and out of circumstances as you actually experience them after separation, and can be tightened up later when you are in a better position really to see what your needs and resources are.

Even though you may be uncertain about what these needs will be, you can try to take into consideration such things as your children's needs for contact with you, your financial situation, and all the other practical problems of separation. The most important thing is to avoid getting stuck with some rigid plan you can't change later. This precaution includes de facto arrangements as well as formal ones. If you and your wife don't have some kind of understanding that your arrangements can be changed later, it is possible for temporary arrangements based on crisis circumstances and perhaps never even put into words, to become permanent ones unsatisfactory later on.

If your communication stinks, but you both want to be able to talk these matters over, get a counselor, therapist, or reasonably neutral third party to help you work something out. There are going to be areas of disagreement with plenty of strong feelings feeding into them. But if you can agree to work through a third party you'll feel freer to bring up the troublesome areas you need to discuss in spite of the negative feelings.

If one of you feels the need to legalize the agreement, and you aren't going to have custody of the children, make provisions for maximum "visitation" rights. Even if you don't feel able to cope with caring for your children at the moment, it's a lot easier to beg off these responsibilities temporarily than to try to increase "visiting" time later on.

Almost anything you and your wife are able to agree on can be built into the separation agreement, including flexibility. One agreement we know of, for instance, stipulates specific visiting times but also states that the father is entitled to extra weekends with the kids which can be decided on at the time. Other agreements guarantee "reasonable" periods of time with the children during the summer, holidays, and at other times as agreed upon by both parents. As this terminology suggests, the specifics have to be worked out by the parents on an as-needed basis from day to day or week to week. Practically speaking, this is generally the way things work even with the most precisely structured agreements.

We'll go into some of the considerations which might govern your choices in the matter of custody or visitation rights later. For the moment our intent is only to alert you to some of the potential long-term effects of the decisions or actions taken by you at the time of separation and to encourage both you and your wife to take an active part in deciding how things will go for you and your family after you have parted.

The more you are able to design an agreement suited to you and your family's needs before the process gets into legal hands, the better off you'll be. Once you get caught up in the legal merry-go-round you might find all the things you once saw as your natural and unquestioned right, like seeing your children when you want to, making decisions about their care or schooling, and so on, taken from you and decided upon by someone who doesn't even know you or your children.

## Enter Lawyers

All of this talk of optimal ways of working out a separation agreement may be completely useless to you, either because it's too late or because some of the necessary conditions do not obtain. Both parties have to be able to set aside their grievances to some extent to work out a mutually acceptable agreement. If the way you go about preparing to separate is one-sided and covert, or particularly destructive, one or the other of you may feel so deceived or damaged that there is no question of co-operation at least in the short run. The "wronged" party may in fact feel obliged to be vindictive and punishing at every opportunity. Lawyers are ideal executioners of this kind of policy.

In all fairness to lawyers, however, more often than not the "executioner" is frequently a champion of one party or the other, providing muscle to protect his or her client from the irresponsibility or arrogance of the former marriage partner. A balance of power is needed if fair bargaining is to take place and sometimes a lawyer, or two evenly matched lawyers may provide it. If parity must be reached in this way, so be it. We think it's a lousy way, but there are times when it is necessary and can work.

Although some people are able to handle their own separations and divorces, most make use of a lawyer or get legal advice at some point; others may be able to deal with each other only through legal advocates. Regardless of when, or for what purpose these professionals are consulted, it is important to realize that legal formulas are limited. Once divorce and separation agreements are put down on paper they become frozen in a sense, fixed by the language used, and they can only be altered through expensive and often painful procedures. So it's very important that what is written down is something you'll be able to live with.

Just as the antiquated marriage contract has proven inadequate for the present-day needs of many of us, the general formulas used for separation and divorce are likewise often inappropriate.

Even though it's too late for you to write a better marital agreement you may still have time to write your own ticket for separation or divorce. The more things that you and your wife can work out together before you see a lawyer, the more you can have things your own way, the way that you and your wife think will be best in the long run.

You will also save a lot of money. Legal costs are high and may drain financial resources already badly strained by the need to support two households, an additional car, baby-sitters, and so on. People who are separating seldom think very realistically about how their standard of living will be affected by divorce. You may feel you make enough to afford a really nice, expensive, well-catered divorce until the bills start coming in afterward when you and your wife have divided the income between two households.

Even if you are very angry with one another now, the cost of spitefulness and rancor may be too high a price to pay later in both dollars and in lost co-operation. There are social agencies in most communities that have the counseling facilities to help you work out a mutually acceptable agreement or at least to help you establish basic areas of agreement before you consult a lawyer. These services are usually free or inexpensive, and are aimed at saving your health as well as your money. For people with limited incomes (and this may include one or both of you after you separate!) legal aid services are also generally available at nominal or no cost when you're ready for them.

All this is a way of saying that it is possible to deal with potential sources of discomfort before they actually occur. In addition to undermining an important source of acrimony that could develop around custody of the children, the working out of an agreed-upon plan for sharing responsibility for the children will bring immediate relief, because you will have fulfilled some important aspects of your responsibility to the children.

## Telling the Children

Having some idea of what you are going to do with the children will certainly be helpful when you break the news to them that you're separating. And we do recommend that *both* of you tell the children, together if possible. If you've usually left it up to your wife to communicate things to the children, now is the time to break that pattern. It's important that you talk to them personally if you are to help them come to some understanding about what is going to happen to *your* relationship with them when you split up with their mother. Your wife can't very well speak for you on this matter.

She may have to if you leave without recognizing that separation from your wife will also mean at least partial separation from your children. We know recognition of this fact brings pain you'd probably like to avoid, but you'll have to face your losses at some point if you are to regain contact with your children (or establish contact for the first time, which happens in some cases). Pretending that neither you nor the kids will be losing anything may avert grief momentarily, but hanging onto this belief too long may lead to permanent loss instead of a momentary one. We'll talk more about this later.

Having specific plans formulated, guaranteeing continuity of your contact with your children, will make news-breaking and parting a great deal easier for you and your kids. It will also make things easier for your wife, knowing when and how you will resume your share of responsibility for the kids.

Naturally, the older your children are, the easier it will be to communicate to them what is happening. If, as is usually the case, it is you who will be leaving home, tell them where you are going and how you can be reached. Write down the address and phone number for them if they are old enough to read and give it to each of your children personally. Assure them that you will get in touch with them as soon as you can and do so at your first opportunity. If you know for certain when you will see them next, give them the details.

Explain to them why you are leaving as simply as possible. As we've mentioned before, it's probably not a good idea to go into a lot of detail, but don't be surprised if they have some questions of their own. Try to answer these questions as openly and honestly as you can, but remember to keep it short and simple. This is no time for elaborate theories.

On the whole you'll probably find that your children can readily accept fairly global and rather matter-of-fact statements to the effect that you and their mother find it difficult to continue living with one another. They should have had ample examples of that fact already. They shouldn't have much trouble understanding that it is a problem between the two of you if you present it to them that way. Most kids have experienced some kind of falling out with a friend for personal reasons and should be able to accept your split as belonging to the two of you without having to feel involved or responsible for your separation. The fact that you will also be leaving them temporarily can then be acknowledged as a consequence of a falling out with their mother, placing your departure in a context they can understand even though they may not like it.

If you have worked out arrangements for seeing the kids, or for custody and visitation rights, let the kids know what they are. Again, don't get technical or legalistic with them, unless they ask for details. Just tell them what it means in concrete terms, such as: "You and your brother will be staying with your mom until I move into the apartment. Then you will come over to my place every other weekend, starting as soon as I move my stuff in, and I hope that we can manage it so that you'll be able to stay over on Wednesday nights as well." In short, try to provide as much structure for your kids as possible.

But in doing so don't make any promises you can't keep, even if you think it will make them feel happy at the moment. They'll tend to take as firm commitments statements you only intended as wishes for the future. In the example above, for instance, they're likely to hear the statement, "I hope that we can manage it so that you'll be able to stay over Wednesday nights" as a definite promise, and they are likely to sit around waiting for you to show the very next Wednesday. So, even though you may want to keep your own hopes up, try not to get theirs going unrealistically. If you really aren't sure you'll be able to make it, make certain that your children understand that.

However they first receive the news, your kids will be looking to you for reassuring signs of love and caring. Any way that you are able to express it, however awkwardly or indirectly, will be received by them at some level. If you are able to communicate your warmth and love directly, holding them close and speaking to each of them personally, that's great. But if you're uptight, distant, or guilt-ridden, because of the pickle you're in, you probably won't be Mister Warmth for a while. Tell them what you can anyway, and don't worry. If there's caring in you, your kids will spot it even if you don't at the moment.

## Telling Your Parents

Telling your parents about your separation could be even trickier than telling your children, depending to some extent on their investment in your marriage and your kids. It's important to remember that your parents are also your children's grandparents. They may be hard hit by news which threatens their relationship with their grandchildren, and they may feel entitled to have a say in the matter beyond what you anticipate. This being the case, they will probably want a certain degree of input into matters that affect your welfare and that of their grandchildren, not all of which you may be prepared to receive or tolerate.

If you do anticipate strong reactions from your parents on this basis, it may be best to hold off telling them until you've worked out as many details of the separation as possible. That way you'll be able to offer them some assurance that the kids are all right, that both you and their daughter-in-law have made adequate plans for their care, and most importantly for the grandparents, that they will still be able to see the kids as often as they did before. If in spite of these assurances you still end up feeling bombarded by a lot of unhelpful and disagreeable input from your parents, be prepared to set their concerns aside until you can afford to deal with them. You are going to be busy enough without having to attend to your parents' needs.

If, on the other hand, you are sure that your folks will be fine, and will be more prepared to offer you the support you need than to demand reassurances for themselves, by all means let them know right away. Even if you aren't sure your parents will be interested in what's going on, don't be afraid to ask if you need help or advice. You might be agreeably surprised.

## Telling Your Friends

Friends, at least some of them, are more likely to be of immediate help to you than parents simply because they are usually closer, both in proximity and in their awareness of who you are at this moment in your life. Your friends are also more likely to have some idea that your marriage has been heading for trouble. So, it probably will be easier to break the news to them than to your parents. Keeping your friends abreast of the situation may also give them some clues as to how they might best go about helping you.

Not all of your friends are going to come through for you, of course. Many of your married friends will be frightened of contagion. Seeing your difficulties, they may begin to wonder about the stability of their own relationship, and will probably have to spend some time checking their own boat for leaks before welcoming survivors aboard.

Some married friends will drop away simply because they were tied to you only as a couple and not as individuals. Others may take sides, and oddly enough, you may find those who side with you more of a liability than an asset, especially if you are interested in having an amicable rather than a combative separation.

The friends who do hang in there with you need to be husbanded wisely. You don't want to place burdens on them that they can't reasonably handle or that they will resent later on, because you are going to be needing them to help you over the long haul as well as right now. Besides, if you're a friend of theirs you have obligations too, to care about their well-being, even though you may be needy as hell at the moment.

So don't set your friends up as nurses or judges, champions or messenger boys. Don't expect them to join you in attacks against your wife, and try not to get paranoid or hurt if they don't agree with everything you do. You are going to need someone who cares about you and about how things go for you, not someone who is as crazy as you are at the moment. You really don't want everyone jumping in your boat with you and sinking it.

When the time comes these friends will be able to help you by being there when you're lonely, when you need to work something out in your mind, and when you're missing the kids or catastrophizing about your life. They'll help you stay grounded. And, if you aren't too much of a pain in the ass, they may even put you up for a while when you separate.

## Getting a Place to Live

When you leave home, and it's the father who usually has to, you're going to have to have a place to live, and it sure is nice if you can stay with friends until you get more permanent quarters. Hotels and motels are such lonely, impersonal places, and friends can be such a comfort at this time. If a motel is all that is possible, it may be a good place to grieve or fume in privacy for a while, but get on the phone to someone if you feel depressed or lonely. Breaking your isolation in this way, through contact with your friends or your kids, will offset the sense of helplessness that can creep up on you if you are living alone the first few weeks of separation.

If your departure isn't too precipitous, you may have a chance to look around for more adequate and more permanent accommodations before moving out. It is important what these quarters look like, because when you are vulnerable, your surroundings can make a big difference in how you feel. If you have the time and money, we suggest shopping around to find a place you really like, and one that is large enough for the kids as well as yourself. Avoid small, bachelor-type apartments if you can, because when the kids come over you're going to need some room to breathe.

You might want to take the children into account too when you consider location. A place fairly near their school, for example, would allow them to walk to school as well as making it easier for them to visit you from their mother's or just to drop in for "unofficial" visits. This kind of location also has the advantage of being near their friends, especially friends they make at school.

But if you feel you really want to get away from the old neighborhood and the discomfort of being near your wife, and you are willing to put up with some of the logistical difficulties, by all means do so. You can still take your children's need for playmates into consideration by choosing a place where there are other kids. Swinging bachelor pads in high-rise apartments may have a romantic appeal, but then you'll have to be prepared to be an all-round playmate to your kids as well as papa.

But we anticipate ourselves, perhaps. You may not be ready to think about anything at the moment of separation except getting out. All this talk about setting up house with your kids may sound bizarre and madly irrelevant to you as you stumble out of the house toward the great unknown. Your own troubles looming before you, or your wild and groovy fantasies, may overshadow any thought of the kids.

# Separation from the Children as Foreground

It would be quite easy for someone with an unsympathetic turn of mind to read what we've said thus far as a kind of fatherly cover-up. In a way it is true. We have gently suggested that a lot of fathers leave their kids behind along with their marriages because they are sort of absent-minded. They are so preoccupied with the crisis of separation and re-entry into the world that they "forget" they are fathers with kids, and only get upset later when they realize they've misplaced their children.

Although this unkind portrayal has its elements of truth, we also know that fathers who are only temporarily amnesic are no problem. Once they've recovered from the crisis they'll be able to focus attention again on their children.

For many fathers, however, even after the dust has settled there is a vague sense of loss and an equally vague sense of responsibility. They feel as if they are "supposed to" see the kids, but beyond some fuzzy idea of duty, they may not quite understand why.

Some fathers may see their kids as almost physical extensions of their ex-wives. They may feel excluded and irrelevant to their children, except perhaps as an economic girder for the maternal nest. Feeling unappreciated and unwanted, they may have no awareness of their importance as fathers.

Separated fathers as a matter of fact tend to underestimate grossly their significance and value to their children, and for good reason. Although we are beginning to make progress toward liberation from the restrictive traditional roles of fathers as breadwinners and mothers as child-rearing members of the family unit, such views are still very much in evidence. We won't go into the politics of this model at the moment, but it's important to understand that its underlying assumptions powerfully govern our perceptions of the world and our conceptions of who we are and what we're here for. In particular, it governs our views of who and what fathers and mothers are and what their respective relationships "should" be to the children.

## Fathers Outside the Family

With the breakdown of the keystone of the model, the family, the traditionally prescribed roles suddenly cease to make sense, and the associated attitudes and expectations become functionally irrelevant. Yet, most of us tend to maintain our role conceptualizations and try to make them work in the vacuum of separation and divorce.

We still tend to think of ourselves as fathers in terms of what that meant in the family. Usually that meant your wife took care of the kids while you went out to work. So, after separation, your ex-wife is still taking care of the kids and you are still helping to support them. The big difference is that you can't take contact with your kids for granted any longer because you won't get to see your children the way you used to. Even if the remoteness of your relationship with your kids never worried you before, after separation the distance from your children may become far too great to ignore. If you want to be close to them, you have to ditch old roles and learn some new ones. And you have to figure out some way of being with your children that doesn't depend on having their mother around to feed and clothe and nurse them. You'll have to become a "mother" to your children as well as a father, performing her roles as well as your own when you're with the kids.

If you were prepared to assume these responsibilities at the outset, chances are you have worked out an agreement involving at least joint custody of the children. If you weren't prepared, either because it had never occurred to you that you might be able to take care of your children as well as your wife does, or because you hadn't as yet acquired the necessary skills at the time you separated, you probably didn't expect or even want partial custody of your children. More likely you assumed she'd care for them and you'd visit them. You hadn't thought such an arrangement might actually upset you, and even when the reality of being separated from your children does hit you you may still be perplexed. What's wrong with the arrangement? Why has it worked out so badly?

## What's Wrong?

In spite of the fact that times are changing, our culture continues to encourage us to misperceive our relevance as fathers and it provides little support for men who assume nurturant roles with their children. We are still told in all kinds of ways that we aren't really needed in the home; we are required in the labor force. We don't "belong" in the home, but on the job. Very few work situations provide for paternal leaves, for instance, or for reduction or flexibility in working hours to allow men to spend more time with their children.

Like most men, separated fathers have bought the old model without question, finding themselves "helplessly" deprived of their children when the model has broken down. Without a new way of conceptualizing their roles with their children, separated fathers simply don't understand what is wrong.

We sense something isn't right about the incomprehensible pain of "losing" our children. But we are often quite unaware of our part in creating and perpetuating our own dilemma. Because of our unexamined assumptions and our training we lose our kids through our own passivity. Neither our culture nor our models take the kids away. Typically, we just let them go!

## Our "Reasons"

We always have our "reasons" for accepting this loss. Consistent with our sense of diminished importance and responsibility, we may see the children's mother as the main person in their lives. Honestly wanting to do what we think is best for our children, we may feel that doing well by them means letting their mother raise them so that the kids have a "family."

We may also attribute all kinds of power to the children's mother. Sometimes we may actually find ourselves afraid to ask for more time with the kids or for more of a role in the lives of our children. We may fear outright rejection as incompetent, irrelevant, or undeserving people, actually believing these things to be true ourselves.

Fear of being justly or unjustly punished by being refused access to the children may also result in self-imposed exile or timidity.

"Don't ask for more," the feeling goes, "because you may lose what you already have if you make her angry."

Feelings of unworthiness, out of guilt about the separation or events leading to the separation, or because of feelings about having been a poor father in the past, may also contribute to passivity. In some cases, loss of the children may actually be experienced as just punishment for these and other real or imagined sins.

Whether out of guilt, antagonism, or some other type of discomfort, avoidance of your former wife may simultaneously cause you to avoid your children simply because they are within her territory. In other instances, having to approach your former wife to get your children may be just too painful.

The temptation to blame your former wife for your avoidance of the children does little good, not only because blame itself is impotent, but because blaming the children's mother is merely a continuation of your focus on her rather than on the kids themselves. You need to be able to see past the discomforts of your relationship with your former wife to appreciate your special relationship with the children.

Practical as well as psychological problems often play an important role in dulling paternal feelings and place hurdles in the way of fathering. The increased financial burdens of separation and divorce, for instance, are normally carried by the children's father. You may be kept too busy trying to meet these obligations to find time for the kids. Even if you don't have to put in overtime or take another job to make ends meet, your job may permit very little free time to be with your children. These financial and work problems not only offer an impediment to your spending time with your kids but further exaggerate the provider-mother model at the heart of the problem.

Physical distance from the children may also play a big part in hampering your chances of fathering, especially if your ex-wife moves to another town with the kids. Nothing brings on feelings of futility and helplessness so dramatically as the idea that your ex-wife may take off with the kids. If your job requires you to relocate or do a lot of traveling, you may feel helpless about seeing your kids because of your own competing demands.

As time goes on, the development of new relationships may also compete for your time and affection. You might find yourself torn between wanting to see and take care of your kids and wanting to spend time with a new friend who may or may not share your interest in the children.

Alternatively, you may become so enamored of the bachelor life that you may find it difficult to give up your "freedom" for the often arduous and mundane responsibilities of fatherhood. Finally, of course, just plain laziness or inertia may get in the way of fathering, involving basic expertise in putting things off or allowing someone else to do the work for you.

As we said, there are a hell of a lot of reasons why fathers who are separated from their children allow fatherhood to slip through their fingers along with the dissolution of their marriage. The idea that this process of letting your children go may after all be "natural" or that gathering your children to your paternal bosom may actually be "unnatural" is of course bullshit. We certainly agree that it isn't easy to continue fathering after separation, but we know it's possible in spite of the difficulties, and we'd be happy with more company.

If you followed our version of the ideal path, coming to some mature agreement with your former wife about sharing responsibility for raising your offspring, great. Forget we said all those other things. We never doubted you for a moment. But if you did go about it all "wrong" and really buggered things up, that's okay too. Read on, the situation is probably salvageable.

## "Losing" Your Children and Finding Them

First of all, if you've become aware that you've left home without the kids, an important change has already taken place. Whatever may have kept you from appreciating your loss of the children has ceased to blind you. Unfortunately, this necessary realization is often accompanied by catastrophic feelings about "losing" your children, which may be equally blinding.

Alarm about not having the kids, or about having lost them permanently, is an extremely common reaction among separated fathers who have had a sort of reawakened awareness of their children. Often these feelings are accompanied by angry feelings that the children's mother is somehow holding the kids for ransom. If you don't pay her child support or alimony, or be nice to her, you won't be able to have the kids this weekend.

This kind of reaction can lead to real trouble if some appreciation of the reality of the situation isn't soon recovered. The circumstances are likely to have changed for the children's mother as well as for yourself, making co-operation in raising the children possible.

Full-time single parenting, for instance, isn't easy, and because it's usually stressful it isn't often very satisfying either. Consequently, your ex-wife may be a lot more willing to let you share the kids than she was before, especially if she needs and wants more time to herself. Keeping the kids from seeing their father out of spite, or for whatever reason, may have lost importance for her, and few mothers want to assume the responsibility for depriving their children of their father. So more than likely, your ex-wife will be ready to renegotiate visiting arrangements.

If you've had a change of heart about the kids, your ex-wife won't know it unless you tell her in some way. Renegotiating may be difficult, particularly if your communication with your former wife is poor or nonexistent. She may wonder if your interest is really genuine or simply a continuation of the avarice both of you may have displayed when you were fighting over material possessions at the time of separation. It will help if you've been able to make this discrimination for yourself. Becoming clear about what your own motives are in wanting the kids and being able to communicate them can change the situation into one in which co-operation is possible. Here's a personal example.

Meditating in his own catastrophizing way about being unfairly deprived of "his" kids, Dick began to notice something funny about his complaining. His children sounded like lost possessions rather than kids. His outraged complaints about being dispossessed seemed directed by an eye glued to his belly button rather than on the children themselves.

It began to dawn on Dick that the children weren't his or hers for that matter. They didn't belong to anyone. His catastrophizing seemed to be about a loss of ownership that had never been valid to begin with. He still had a relationship with each of his kids that no one could take away from him, nor did anyone really seem interested in doing so. His love for them was still intact and there was nothing to prevent him from being the best father he could when he and the kids were together.

As this view of his kids as owned objects began to drop away, awareness of them as persons began to re-emerge. His thoughts were for Robbie and Samantha and what they were feeling and what they needed. Lifting his eyes from his navel to their faces, he saw they were looking back at him! He hadn't lost the kids; he'd found them.

That's what this book is all about, the rediscovery of our children and of ourselves as fathers.

# Toward a New Way of Being a Father

It's very easy to write about the business of being a separated father from a position of righteousness, responsibility, fulfillment, and even fun. It would be easy to pretend we've never had doubts about caring for our children or about our ability to care for them, or for that matter, that we always feel certain about the things that we do now. But our beginnings as separated fathers were not as simple or virtuous as all that. The process of getting in tune with our new roles was no different than for most separated fathers, involving lots of mistakes and pain, a variety of discomforts and uncertainty, and finally some degree of success and satisfaction.

So before talking about why we think men "ought to" continue fathering after separation, we thought it might be worth while to begin by describing many of the "rotten" attitudes that are often characteristic starting points for the newly separated father. These attitudes, by the way, are very common and are quite natural considering the upbringing most of us have experienced in our culture. Although they are often barriers to fathering after separation, these attitudes can be overcome, and they needn't prevent any man from becoming a "virtuous" and terrific father. As a first step, though, let's have a hypothetical father (a composite of many friends and clients we've known) tell us why he *doesn't* want to do any fathering after separation.

## Why I Don't Want to Be a Father

What do you mean, I ought to be taking care of my kids? I'm having enough trouble right now just taking care of myself. Don't you think I want to be a good father? Okay. I know I have some obligation to them. But how can I take care of them now that I'm separated? I feel like I should be doing something, but what? Maybe it's not such a good idea to try just now. Anyway, it looks like a terrible job and I'm not qualified to do it by myself. Now that we're separated, why should I be expected to take over the responsibility of raising the kids? That's my ex-wife's job, isn't it? And I'm paying her to do it; that's what the support payments are for.

Let's be honest about it. Bringing up kids is a pain in the ass. It takes too much time. It means spending all my free time with them, and I'd rather be golfing, or fishing, or playing poker than horsing around with kids. Why should I give up the few pleasures I have? I work hard for a living and I've got a right to some enjoyment in my life. Besides, my work is more important than taking care of kids. If I don't work, they don't eat.

The kids don't need me anyway. Their mother takes good care of them and they're more interested in her or in playing with their classmates than they are in me. We don't have much in common. I'd probably go nuts hanging around with them all the time. I can't see myself getting into disco dancing or football cards. I'm getting too old to play horsy.

On top of all this, I guess I just wouldn't do a real good job of raising them anyway. What do I know about kids? I don't know how to cook and I certainly don't want to learn. When I get into a supermarket, I'm completely lost. What kinds of things should I buy? What kinds of things do my kids like to eat and what's good for them? I don't want to bust my ass fixing something for some dumb kid who looks like he's going to throw up if he doesn't like what I give him. And boy, are they messy and noisy? It's painful enough taking them out to eat, never mind having to listen to them constantly at home.

I don't want to be a maid to my kids, either. Did you ever see what kids can do to a place? They leave their toys and dirty clothes and comic books all over. And forget about trying to get them to make their beds.

Besides, my apartment is too small. There isn't enough room for the kids. If I did keep them overnight, I'd have to drive them to school in the morning. It's a long way, and getting those slow pokes organized early in the morning is no picnic. There aren't any other kids in my neighborhood. Who will they play with? I certainly don't want them hanging onto me all the time.

If I wanted time to myself, and I do, I'd have to find a sitter and I've no idea how to go about that. I don't know anyone with kids old enough to baby-sit. And my girl friend hates kids, or at least she gets sore if I have to pay attention to mine. My kids don't particularly like her, either. I don't want to get caught in the middle of a fight between them, having to be a referee or to listen to the lousy things they say about each other. And I need some time alone with my girl friend, too.

The more I see those kids the more I have to see their mother. I got separated because I didn't want to see her any more. It's just too painful having to talk to her and she nags me about things. She criticizes how I take care of the kids and I resent it; even if she's often right. I hate being ridiculed constantly. Let her take care of them if she knows so much about it. Besides, as I said, that's what I'm paying her for. Why give her money if I'm going to be feeding them, buying them clothes, and housing them myself? She doesn't give me anything.

So tell me, why should I take care of the kids? They wouldn't appreciate it anyway. They take everything for granted. Give them something and all they do is ask for more. They're spoiled.

I don't want to have to spend time disciplining them. I don't want to yell at them or have them mad at me. I want things to be okay and peaceful in this house. I've had enough troubles. If I have to spend time with the kids, I'd like a little appreciation for it instead of more crap.

Being a father is a lousy, unrewarding job. Who needs it?

## But I Don't Feel Right About It

It's hard to argue with these complaints. Many of them are true to some extent. Why would anyone want the job of raising kids? Looking at it from a purely objective standpoint, it really is a difficult, time-consuming, and draining task, with little apparent reward or recognition. So why have women usually been expected to do most of the child rearing? It isn't because they have special powers or capacities or strengths that men do not have. It's not because they are necessarily more dedicated, or because they have nothing else of importance to do in the world. And it's certainly not because of "maternal instinct," whatever that is.

Granted that it is women who spend nine months carrying their babies in their growing bellies, thinking about it, planning for it, preparing themselves for "motherhood," and who bear the discomfort and pain and triumph of childbirth, and who nurse the infant in its first days. And granted that these compelling and absorbing experiences culminate a lifetime of social learning and expectancies preparing women to care for their children. It's no wonder that women (and others) see the babies as *theirs* and accept their own ascendancy in the area of child care.

It would be fatuous to suggest that women do not receive extremely persuasive indoctrination and training in the task of raising children as a result of these intensive experiences. It is also very clear that men would have to undertake some very special learning experiences if they wanted to catch up to women. (That's one reason for this book.) When we look at the complaints of our hypothetical father, however, we are left with the impression that women not only have a terrific head start, but that they must also have some ineffable gifts and powers enabling them to handle all of the difficulties of child rearing. (And, by implication, that men are bound to be weak, frail, and incompetent in this area.) This simply isn't so.

Arguments that biological or god-given powers are the reasons why mothers *rather than* fathers should take care of children are highly suspect. Biologically speaking, having babies is certainly a woman's province. Taking care of them is not. Given some opportunity to catch up, men can learn to do the job equally well.

Our hypothetical father might be able to recognize this once he begins to hear the defensiveness in his own protests and arguments against fathering. Eventually he might be able to admit that he's afraid of the responsibilities of fathering, or that because he doesn't really want to do the job, he has become good at dreaming up reasons why he "can't" or why his ex-wife should.

Feelings of defensiveness are characterized by the whine in your voice as you underline the reasons you shouldn't take care of the kids, or the cornered feeling of resentment, of being bugged or pushed or "guilt-tripped," even when nobody else may be saying a thing about it except you. These are signs that can help you to see that the position you are defending isn't defensible to yourself. And in the end, you may be able to give full recognition and attention to your own concerns about not participating in raising your children.

## It's a Hard Job

Being a parent *is* a hard job. But that probably isn't a valid reason to avoid it. We often do other jobs that are difficult without thinking twice about it. Parenting is also a thankless job in some ways, but we do lots of things without expecting gratitude. Why should we expect thanks for fathering our children? And from whom?

Assuredly, the stresses of taking care of kids can make you miserable. But suffering isn't a *necessity*. It is only another good sign that you need to learn something.

There are tricks to this trade (timing, planning ahead, rule setting, and just plain relaxing) and special resources (baby-sitters and other helpers) that can take some of the stress out of child rearing. We offer some of these tips later on. There are also attitudinal changes that are part of the catching up, which can smooth things out for you. Learning to value the *process* by which children learn things, for instance, rather than just pushing for quick achievement of goals can help you find the patience to enjoy your children's accomplishments rather than getting uptight about their shortcomings.

So initial stresses needn't dissuade you from learning new ways of coping with the novelties of the job, or from finding ways of making it not just tolerable, but fun. There's no reason why we fathers can't accept the responsibilities of fathering like any other exciting challenge to our abilities to learn and to be creative.

## What's in It for You?

But why bother? Some fathers may see the whole task of child rearing as unworthy of their efforts and harmful to their social standing. Child care is viewed as a low-status job, "unmanly" in some way, and these fathers may feel other people will look down on them as dupes for taking on such an odious task when they don't have to. One thing is certain, whether you're looked upon with scorn for being a father to your children or not, taking care of your kids isn't something you can do for praise or high regard. The rewards have to come from within, not from other, essentially disinterested people.

You can know the importance of what you are doing even if others do not. There's certainly no reason for you to accept the defensiveness of other people about raising kids as valid criteria for yourself to follow. And there is something deeply satisfying about finding the personal integrity to do the job despite criticism or the lack of external rewards. As your own awareness of what you are doing grows, so will your pride and self-respect.

In other words, accepting the role and responsibility of a father would be an affirmation of yourself and your strength and not a confirmation of foolhardiness or weakness. And the things you'd have to learn would enhance your competence to take care of yourself as well as your children. You would begin to enjoy self-reliance in the business of everyday living rather than having to depend on someone else to take care of you, or to take care of your kids *for you*.

## What's in It for Your Kids?

You may get something out of it besides misery and scorn, but how about your kids? Are you really important to them? What can you bring to them that their mother or teachers or some other guy can't? Will it really hurt them if you aren't around?

To be sure, some of your functions as a father may be replaceable, but *you* aren't. Think about it. What would your kids miss if you weren't around? What kinds of things have they yet to learn from you, and about you? In answering, try to remember you aren't just a role to them, you're somebody special. And you will always be special to them, because you're their father, even though they may not know who you are yet! It takes time for children to get to know their dads. Will your kids have that chance? Will they get to know what you do at work, or how you are with people outside the family? Will they get to understand and appreciate your values and attitudes?

If you ask yourself these questions and answer them honestly, you're bound to notice that your children *would* lose some important things, things that are unique to you as a person, not just because you're their dad.

## But What's So Important About Fathers?

If you are still uncertain about your importance to your children as a father, don't put it down as merely your personal problem. Don't think that your uncertainty means there is something uniquely wrong with you because you're separated or divorced or because you don't seem to have some strong and immediate sense of your importance as a father. *Most of the men in our society do not know their own importance as fathers.*

In promoting awareness of what they call *Father Power,** Henry Biller and Dennis Meredith emphasize this point again and again: "The principal danger to fatherhood today . . . is that fathers do not have the vital sense of father power that they have had in the past. Because of a host of pressures from society, the father has lost the confidence that he is naturally important to his children—that he has the power to affect children, guide them, help them grow. He isn't confident that *fatherhood is a basic part of being masculine and a legitimate focus of his life.*" And they aren't talking about separated fathers, they're talking about fathers who are living in intact households!

You were hardly alone if you didn't appreciate your relevance as a father while you were married. If now, as a result of separation and divorce, you have begun to wonder about how important you might be to your children, you have come a long way. You are among the few who are even seriously considering the question, and you may be on the way to experiencing the answer first hand.

The sad thing is the fact that we may have had to go through the pain of a separation from our children to begin to appreciate our own value as fathers. Why were we so unaware before? Why is it so hard to grasp now?

In good part, the answer is that we've been *trained* to believe that child rearing is a mother's job, not a father's. The "experts," authorities, teachers, and other information sources (including our own fathering models), who might have told us otherwise, all tend to see child rearing as a woman's province just as you have. They've had almost nothing to say about fathers as a consequence. Take a look at

* Henry Biller and Dennis Meredith, *Father Power* (New York: Anchor Press/ Doubleday, 1975), p. 7.

any of the magazines or newspaper articles dealing with children, for instance. They're almost exclusively written for women, appearing in women's magazines and in women's sections of newspapers.

Even more importantly, the influence of these attitudes is as profound as it is unappreciated. The motherhood and apple-pie view permeates all of our institutions, seriously affecting our lives. Why do you suppose the courts so consistently discriminate against fathers in divorce cases, for example? It certainly isn't because men *can't* do practically anything a woman can in caring for children, or because men are consistently undeserving of the chance. We believe the main reason is that men aren't *expected* to participate in raising their children.

If we are ignorant of child-rearing skills or short on experience, it isn't because we can't learn. It's because we have never been expected to learn. On the contrary, doing things like washing dishes or setting the table are still considered woman's work, and husbands (or children) who do it are often seen as "helping mother out" rather than simply doing a chore that needs doing by someone.

Men aren't handicapped as parents because they lack "maternal instincts." Nurturance isn't a "feminine" possession any more than assertiveness is a "masculine" one. Men are potentially as well equipped to be parents as women are, except for the attitudes and beliefs which stand in the way of their learning.

There are many social, political, and economic reasons for playing down the importance of fathering as well as for the enormous investment in persuading women that their role is to raise children. But we don't want to get side-tracked on the politics that have led to our present imbalances in parenting. Our main point is to emphasize that you are important to your children. They need fathering.

## Fathering Makes a Difference

In summarizing the research literature on father absence and father neglect, Biller and Meredith describe some of the profound effects on children that are directly related to the adequacy or inadequacy of the fathering they have received. While fathers are popularly viewed as useless creatures around infants, for example, and may even be bounced from the nursery, there is evidence to suggest that infants who receive close fathering are better prepared for the world than those with more distant or absent fathers. These kids find periods of separation from their parents much easier to accept, are less afraid of strangers, and are more exploratory of their environments than kids with less adequate fathering.

With a father around as well as a mother, infants have two people to relate to and learn about rather than one, and this makes an important difference. The way a father handles his children will be different from the way their mother holds them or plays with them, for instance, and for this and countless other reasons, you provide your kids a breadth of experience from which they'll benefit.

Later in your children's lives you'll be able to contribute importantly to their sex education in unique ways. Not only will you provide a role model for your sons and be able to reassure them about themselves sexually in ways their mother cannot, but as the first man in your daughter's life, you can make a big difference in how she sees men and herself in relation to them.

By being a nurturant father you present to both your daughters and sons a model of men as nurturant beings, making it easier for them to learn broader roles later in life. Watching what you do as a separated father, seeing you assume responsibilities and perform tasks that cut across traditional sex roles, may play an important part in breaking down some of the existing stereotypes we've talked about. You will also be able to turn your own early training to good stead by encouraging your children of both sexes to develop themselves in areas traditionally identified as "masculine": achievement, assertiveness, independence, enjoyment of physical activity, strength, and so on.

You, as well as their mother, can have an impact on how the children see themselves, on the development of their self-respect, self-confidence, and feeling of worth. How you see your kids and what you say to them will play a big role in who and what they become later in life.

Surprising as it may seem, even intellectual functioning seems to be affected by fathering or its absence. In studies cited by Biller and Meredith, for example, kids with interested fathers had an advantage in analytical ability and problem solving over kids without adequate fathering.

And of course there are the obvious kinds of things that you can teach your children. Things like fixing a bicycle tire, building something, or playing ball, all things that mothers might be able to do but probably haven't learned because they *too* have been constricted by societally-imposed roles.

Because of your own upbringing, you may be more interested in playing games with the kids, encouraging them to learn spelling or mathematics in the process. Preschoolers can get a start at counting by playing Go Fish with you perhaps and school kids may sharpen up their spelling and vocabulary competing with you at Scrabble.

If you take a direct hand in encouraging your children with their schoolwork, you may also be helping to offset the imbalance that occurs in the earliest grades as a result of the preponderance of women teachers. We'll have more to say about this later.

Besides all these obvious advantages, there are more subtle benefits that active fathering provides. As Biller and Meredith point out, fathers are often a guard against overmothering, smothering, or even symbiotic relationships that might develop between mother and child. It's common enough to see mothers turn to their children for support, comfort, and love when the children's father has left the household. Natural as this may be for any human being, it can easily become unhealthy for everyone concerned. Continued involvement of the father with his children will help to offset this tendency and will also give the children's mother a chance to find other sources of adult support while her ex-husband is caring for the children.

A feature of special importance to the separated father is that continuance of contact with his children will enable him to define himself and his relationship with them, rather than allowing his former wife to do the defining for him. Even under the best circumstances in intact families definitions of the father by the children's mother will be biased, inaccurate, and probably stereotyped according to her own social learning. And the best of conditions seldom exist for the separated and divorced. Mothers may present extremely derogatory views of men in general to their kids and perhaps scathing ones of you in particular. This might be difficult for you to handle, but without you around to define yourself to them your kids might have an uphill fight with cynicism and doubt about you and men in general that only a great deal of relearning could offset later in life.

There is good reason, then, to believe that your presence as a father is important to the health and development of your children. But before you get overwrought with guilt as a separated father, thinking about how you may have damaged your kids by "abandoning" them, you'd better get this whole business into proper perspective.

Although there is no doubt that separation and divorce are major causes of father absence and neglect, the problems we've mentioned are only part of a broader problem of neglect of fatherhood in general. As Biller and Meredith emphasize, chronic neglect of children by their fathers is the rule in intact families. Most fathers simply have very little regular, close contact with their children. Fathers who ultimately become separated are probably among this majority to begin with, and like most men do not really know what a father is or can be. Unaware of their own value and importance to their children beforehand, how can they realize how much their kids will need them after separation?

Relegating himself to the dust heap as a husband, it is all too easy for the separated father to do likewise with himself as a father. But, if he feels like a failure as a father, he has lots of company, and not just because he is separated or divorced. Like so many fathers in our society, he may have allowed his job as a father to slip out of his grasp long before troubles with his wife began.

Most fathers never catch on. But because your status dramatically changes with respect to the kids upon separation, you're in a better position to become aware of your importance than fathers still ensconced in the traditional roles in the family. Just as women are often roused from apathy about their rights as persons by divorce, so too do many men become aware of their rights as parents. It's often a slow process. Fathers are often confused at first by their tendency to attribute the pain of "losing" their kids to their own culpability in "leaving" them. They may never question this assumption unless they become aware of the unfair and unhealthy discrimination that operates against fathers, a discrimination which expects, almost demands, that you leave your children if you leave your wife.

Rather than protesting and fighting for our rights as parents, when we do ask for more of a role it is often done apologetically, which is absurd. No one would think of questioning a mother's right to take care of her children. Yet we're expected to prove ourselves worthy of parenthood if we get it into our minds that we wish to father our own kids. We lack confidence in ourselves as parents. We turn to others for judgments about our capability to raise our children, and often the people to whom we turn are as prejudiced against fathering as we are.

How many judges, lawyers, and marriage counselors do you suppose are really aware of the importance of fathering? How many are free of society's false beliefs about fathers and their children? It is actually you who will probably be the first to notice that there is something dreadfully wrong with our rules and expectations, and in that sense, it is you who will become the authority on the subject and on whom our society must ultimately depend for appropriate leadership and change. It is the hungry who recognize the need for food, not the well fed.

You can best begin to change the rules by beginning to father your children, learning what you *can do* as a separated father rather than being put off by what you "can't" or aren't supposed to be able to do. And we do mean learning. Because if you haven't been aware of your importance up to now, you are bound to have a lot of catching up to do. Don't let that put you off. Have respect for yourself having to learn under difficult circumstances. It's hard to unlearn old patterns and take on new ones, especially during the turmoil associated with separation, but you can do it. Be a good, supportive, and encouraging person to yourself rather than a critical taskmaster. Recognize that you aren't likely to comprehend all the issues right from the start. In your head you may grasp the idea of being a father as a good idea, but chances are it will take some time and actual successful experiences of fathering for you to feel in your guts the knowledge of your importance as a father. So give yourself a chance.

After you've left to set up a home on your own is a hell of a time to find out you are important to your kids. But better late than never is not only trite, in this case it's true. If you're annoyed or angry about it, fine. You'll probably need a little zip in you to go about recovering some of your rights and responsibilities as a father.

# Custody and Visitation Rights

Throughout this book you'll notice that we use the word "visit," stemming from the term "visitation rights," which is all that remains of a father's rights to his children after a court "awards" full custody to their mother. It's a galling term for any father (or mother) to use in describing his time with his children. It's as if he has become an uncle or grandfather to his own kids. (And "Uncle Daddy" isn't very funny, even when used ruefully.)

Because your former wife legally "owns" the children if she has been granted complete custody, she has an incredible amount of control over your access to them. Even though the divorce decree spells out at least a minimal amount of time you are allowed to spend with your kids, your ability to exercise your rights is ultimately dependent on the good will of your former wife. There are all kinds of ways she can interfere with your seeing the children if she wants to, sometimes deliberately and sometimes because she thinks that it is in the "best interests" of the children. She may feel a sniffle is reason enough to keep them home when they are supposed to be seeing you, and there may be nothing you can do about it. If she is angry with you and simply refuses to let you see the children it could take a lot of time and trouble and money for you to get to see your children again, because she has custody.

Although there are all too many instances in which control over the children is deliberately used as a weapon against the father, more commonly interference comes in subtler and less deliberate forms. Mothers are frequently unaware of when they are abusing their power over your contacts with the children, and they generally have little idea of the potential impact such actions may have on you and the kids. Mothers often assume that they are totally responsible for the health and welfare of the children once you are separated. As a consequence, they may not only criticize the way you care for the children but they may try to establish rules for doing so in much the same way as they would for a housekeeper or baby-sitter. Being treated in this way is humiliating and frustrating for the separated father. As one alarmed and outraged father put it, "I feel like I have to lease the kids from my wife, now. And if she doesn't like the way I handle them, she can cancel my lease anytime."

This kind of infuriating and myopic maternalism may be expressed in apparently benign ways with the same devastating effects. Thanking a father for "taking care of the kids," for instance, may sound nice and may reflect genuine appreciation, but it also conveys the assumption that the father is a mere baby-sitter. It ignores the fact that they are his children as well as hers and that his contacts with them as a father are quite as valid and important as hers are as a mother.

It's not surprising that fathers often behave oddly under these conditions, with "inexplicable" rages or undiplomatic and "paranoid" attacks, or with depression and helpless withdrawal from their children. Custody decisions that reduce them to mock parents, stripping them of acknowledgment and respect for their dignity as fathers, open separated fathers not only to potential abuses of power at the hands of the children's mother, but also to their own reactions to vulnerability. The anxiety and frustration which these circumstances may engender create a poor climate for co-operative and effective parenting, and make for an uphill battle for separated fathers who still want to be fathers.

It would be tempting to react to these conditions by fighting for complete custody of the children. We don't recommend it. Kids need mothers as well as fathers, and men are as subject to the misuse of power as women. Our recommendation is for joint custody, whenever possible. We think continuation of joint responsibility for the children is a worth-while and workable idea. We use the word continuation even though equal sharing of responsibility for parenting isn't generally present in most families. But we would like to encourage truly co-equal parenting after separation, even if it did not exist before. To this end, it is extremely important for fathers separated from their children as a result of separation and divorce to become aware of their importance to them, to re-establish a relationship with each child, and to resume (or begin) fathering.

In recommending joint custody (responsibility), we're interested in promoting satisfaction for everyone concerned, not merely in obtaining justice for justice's sake and certainly not for the sake of male ownership or dominance. In addition to the fact that children need mothers as well as fathers, we have good reason for not urging a fight for full custody.

Studies have shown that while fathers with complete custody may report relief from many of the problems we've mentioned, they also complain about all of the problems of single parents. These surveys report that satisfaction is, in fact, highest for separated fathers who have their kids about half the time and that fathers who have their children full time or very little are generally not satisfied with the arrangement.

We know that the ideal situation of joint custody, which we recommend, is still the exception in our society. As things stand now, divorced mothers generally are awarded custody of the children while fathers receive the bits and pieces of visiting rights. The kids live with their mothers and visit their fathers for relatively short periods of time. Because this is the way things are at present and because separated fathers need to be able to cope with things as they find them, we will write from this standpoint. But it should be clear by now that we don't like it, and we will press for change.

## How Much Time Is Enough?

When negotiating visiting rights, how then do you decide how much time is enough? And enough time for whom? There are a number of different perspectives from which you may ask the question: from your own perspective as an individual with a life to lead, or from the standpoint of a father who wants to be a parent. Do you ask the question from the point of view of your children or from that of your ex-wife? Do you take into consideration the needs of your present woman friend or mate, and the wishes of your parents and others, or not? Do these different perspectives coincide? And if not, how do you reconcile the differences? These certainly aren't easy questions to answer.

Yet satisfactory decisions will hinge on the answers to these questions. You can't very well neglect other perspectives in favor of your own, because your own happiness and peace of mind depend to some extent on the well-being of the other people in your life. Your own personal needs probably include wanting your children to be happy, and wanting to see that they receive the fathering they require. And you will also need to maintain good relationships with people who are of importance to this task, particularly the children's mother. At the same time, you may want to enjoy the other relationships that sustain and nourish you—with your woman friend or your new wife, your parents, friends, and so on. As a consequence you'll probably have to take all of these perspectives into account to find satisfying answers.

The individuals who represent these other perspectives also have their own ways of pressing their viewpoints on the question of time. Your kids, having no inclination to worry about conflicts with anyone else's needs, may want you to spend more time with them than you feel is available. Spontaneous creatures that kids are, they will probably have just as little regard for constraints imposed on you by separation or divorce agreements when proposing things for you to do with them.

Their mother may have other ideas on the matter. The children's needs and yours may very well conflict with her needs for time with them. But mothers usually have little trouble making their demands for time known and respected. Having custody of the children in most instances, they are generally in a much better position than fathers when negotiating for time.

Your position in these negotiations would be strengthened if you could make a good case for the children's needs for a father. Unfortunately, you'll probably tend to focus primarily on your own personal needs for your children instead. It's unfortunate because a personal emphasis reduces your need for the kids, and they for you, to a plea based on humanitarian grounds alone. It may sound nice, but it is a weak position, lacking the clout and validity that an understanding of fathering would bring to the situation. You'll invariably end up saying something like, "Please don't do this to me," when you might otherwise be vigorously and confidently presenting your case as a father.

Your former wife's needs to be a good parent might easily encompass the desire for her children to have a father, but only if she understands the importance of this job to her children. She may want to support your fathering the children if she has confidence in your awareness and ability to do the job. But both her understanding and yours may only come later as a result of experience. When it is established in her mind that you are a good father, and needed by your children, her ideas about how much time the children should spend with you will correspond more closely with your own.

New relationships with other women and new mates often present special difficulties. Usually their primary or sole interest is in you rather than in your children in the beginning. They may have no interest at all in being mothers, and no concern about your children's needs. The demands of your young children for time and attention may mess up their plans and result in a variety of competing pressures on you. Women friends may sometimes seem unsympathetic to fathering, but in all fairness to them, most adults have trouble accepting the disruptive presence of children, especially if they are used to peace and privacy. We'll talk more about this later, but suffice it to say that at best demands for time and attention by your woman friend or new wife may conflict awkwardly with your need to be with your children.

Grandparents, who may demand time with the children, and friends who want you over to dinner without the kids, also ask for consideration. Your work and related demands put limits on your availability to your kids as well. And all of these demands on your time and energy are likely to be rigid and unforgiving until you've established yourself as a separated father with legitimate needs for time with your children.

Being new at this fathering business, you yourself may underestimate the amount of time your children actually need to be with you. Some experts on fathering recommend, for example, that fathers should spend at least an hour or more every day in personal contact with each child, and even more on weekends. But how can the separated father manage to do that?

In the case of children of divorced fathers, these same experts suggest that frequent, short visits are better for the kids than long but infrequent ones. More frequent contacts provide continuity, which is important because young children have such a shortened time sense. They are also better for keeping up with the kids and their rapid changes and for having regular input into their growth and development.

There's certainly no question that optimal fathering would make dad frequently available to his children. But we've already noted that the circumstances of separation and divorce offer no assurance that parents will remain geographically or emotionally close enough to permit it. If one of the parents moves out of town, obviously the only practical arrangements are those long but infrequent visits.

Even if both parents remain in the same city, they would have to live fairly close to each other to permit the father to have frequent contacts with the children. Many divorced couples find such physical proximity stifling. Moreover, accompanying changes in lifestyle or income often necessitate changes in neighborhood for one or both of the parents. So, although it may make a lot of sense for the divorced parents to live near one another, there are usually more reasons why they choose not to.

Naturally, the amount of time that separated fathers devote to their children is governed by a number of factors besides proximity. A commitment to fathering makes a big difference as to whether or not dads will welcome having the kids around a great deal, or be willing to sacrifice their illusions about a free and easy bachelor life and be prepared to make adjustments in their vocational and social lives to accommodate the needs of their children.

Long visits with the children already presuppose a high degree of commitment. It usually means having a place with enough room for the kids to stay overnight, pajamas, toothbrushes, changes of clothes, as well as being willing to transport the kids to school in the morning. Keeping the kids for extended periods of time also demands child care and housekeeping skills and an ability to cook. As we'll see later, it also means finding ways of interacting co-operatively with your former wife in sharing the responsibilities of child rearing.

Reservations about any of these areas can sharply delimit both the frequency and duration of visits with the children. One of the purposes of this book, of course, is to help separated fathers cope with these problems and enable them to spend more time with their kids. These problems aren't insurmountable, but they often look like incredible obstacles.

## Short Visits

One of the roadblocks to fathering stems from the very shortness of our visits with our children. Most separated fathers are Saturday afternoon specialists at first. Even if they see their kids a little more than that, they still tend to avoid overnight visits and full commitment to their roles as fathers. Consequently, they usually see their kids for short periods of time with fairly large gaps between visits (a week is quite a gap for kids and for most fathers).

In our experience, these conditions almost guarantee misery. Short, infrequent visits foster a subtle, insidious discomfort which often makes contact with the children unrewarding, and discourages many fathers from seeing them more frequently. Vague feelings of anxiety, irritation, and resentment may dilute the pleasure of seeing your kids, and parting from them may seem harder and sadder than it ought to, or even too much of a relief.

Despite the passage of time, you may still find yourself vulnerable to the same things over and over again, never building up an immunity to the pain of seeing the kids. Every fleeting visit has a "special" quality that feels unnatural, and the whole process becomes unaccountably stressful. You may start to wonder if it's worth it and begin to let your visits with the children slide, as well as declining additional opportunities to be with them.

Because the demoralizing aspects of short visits are so subtle, it is easy for you to begin to see yourself as a "bad" father who wasn't really cut out to be a father after all. Perhaps, you may think it would be better to cut your losses and your children's instead of subjecting yourselves to excruciating (or boring) visits. Perhaps they would be better off with a more homey and "healthier" family life with their mother.

These are examples of some of the symptoms associated with short, relatively infrequent visits in the first year or two of separation. The demoralizing conditions inherent in these visits create stresses over and above the ones already painfully present by virtue of the separation itself. Adjustments in the length and frequency of your visits can reduce some of this stress, so let's examine both of these features to see what needs to be done.

## Gaps Between Visits

As we have said, there are obvious difficulties with longish gaps between visits. Important developmental changes take place in the lives of youngsters even in the course of a week. It's not only hard to catch up on what happened, but as far as having any input into how the kids grow or what they learn, that time is irretrievably gone. The younger your kids are the more rapid their changes, and the more likely they are to experience a deficit as a result of your absence.

Sensing this, fathers often feel disquieted when they haven't seen their children for a while. In fact, we think fathers often suffer more than the kids because of the time lag. Everyday spats, for example, that arise in the course of a visit may have to wait a week or more for resolution. Children generally forget about these incidents right away, but newly separated fathers often keep themselves on tenterhooks worrying about what their kids think of them after a blowup. These and other kinds of emotional problems that would normally be resolved by everyday contacts within the family can easily get blown out of proportion when they have to wait too long, causing great distress for the separated father.

## Short Visits Are Stressful

A major problem with short visits is the enormous time pressure that fathers experience as they try to squeeze in a good time with the kids, especially if there are long gaps between visits. Short visits allow little time to do anything really wholesome, and often encourage tight, overplanned programs that lack spontaneity, depth, and satisfaction. They tend to make every minute feel terribly precious, putting pressure on fathers to make every moment count. Trying to squeeze a week's worth of love and contact from an afternoon or a day with the children can really be murder.

## Hello, How Are You? Good-by

But there's more to the problem of short visits than the lack of time. The basic structure of any visit affects what goes on in the visit. Some kinds of activities that are necessary parts of any visit demand a portion of the limited time available. And the nature of each of these parts affects the "success" or satisfaction of the visit as a whole.

A visit can be seen, for example, as having three parts: acquaintance renewal ("hello again"), followed by a middle, living-together-again stage, and ending with separation ("good-by again"). The longer the gaps between visits, the more awkward the hello stage will be because there's so much to catch up on. You may also be feeling bad about having missed the kids. Moreover, if the visit is a short one you haven't much time to catch up, and you probably won't want to spend your whole visit doing so. Your kids certainly won't. Unlike adults, children aren't interested in talking about the past; they want to do something with you right now. Yet, if you fill up the time with things to do, you may lose any chance of discovering "what's new" with your kids.

Short visits aren't as much of a problem if you see your kids fairly often. If the gaps between visits aren't too great, you begin to approach the normal situation; there's little to catch up on and you can get on with what you want to do together without further ado.

The other end of the visiting sandwich is good-by. The stress or poignancy of each parting will depend in part on how long it's been since you last saw each other and how long it will be until next time. It also depends on how well this visit went. Did you catch up enough to feel you know them again? Did you have fun together? Did you have an opportunity to do some fathering or were you only a clown and a chauffeur?

Considering how stressful the two ends of a visit can be, what is the middle going to be like? For one thing, we know it's going to be short—even shorter because of the time taken up by the beginning and end. In short (if you'll pardon a pun), these short visits are all out of whack. There's a disproportionate amount of hello and good-by without enough of the relaxing middle stage of living together. There's not enough meat in the sandwich. The stresses of getting acquainted with each other again and of parting aren't offset by the comforts and rewards of ordinary living. That comfortable feeling of living in the present, free from concern about the past or the future, simply isn't easy to achieve, because you've just greeted each other and will soon have to separate again.

Because it is difficult just to pick up again where you left off, each visit tends to feel like a new event rather than being familiar. As a result, neither you nor your children can relax and take each other for granted very easily. In fact, these conditions actually create a background of tension against which ordinary events are bound to appear even more dramatic and stressful than usual.

It's rather like trying to live with a persistent noise in the background. You may get used to it enough to "forget" that it's there, but

then you may begin to attribute some of its effects on you, like irritability and distractedness, to other things. Unless you take this noise
into account, you won't understand why you feel so strongly about a
lot of things.

## Our Existential Situation

Yet, the situation isn't necessarily all bad. Separation forces
us into an existential situation with our kids; it jacks up our
awareness to an almost acute state of discomfort. The unfamiliar ex-
citement of "seeing" our children contrasts sharply with the normal
ease (or dullness) of familiarity, which often allowed us to take our
kids for granted.

Now, every contact, every touch, smile, or argument with our kids
*is* special—at least for a while. You may actually find some redeem-
ing features in this miserable situation if you think about it this way.
We don't want to romanticize these visits, but some of us may need
to wake up to the preciousness of our time together with our children. We're reminded of Thornton Wilder's *Our Town,* a play in
which a young girl returns after her death for a visit to her past. To
her dismay she discovers that the people she supposed herself close
to—her parents—had actually been too busy and self-absorbed really
to see or touch her.

By accepting your existential situation with your children you may
be able to cope with some of the stresses of separation from them
and begin to appreciate the preciousness of your visits with them.
You can't have your children forever. That's the existential situation
all parents must learn to accept. The kids grow up, leaving you by
degrees—going off to school to learn from other adults, finding new
friends to hang out with, and finally, leaving home to start their own
lives.

For fathers who are completely cut off from their children by divorce, or for those who think they are, the fact that kids grow up
may actually bring some measure of hope, allowing these fathers to
look forward to the day when their children are old enough to make
their own decisions about being with their dad.

But most separated fathers still have a chance to maintain a relationship with their children. They may not welcome this head start in
facing their existential dilemma, but they may succeed in adapting to

its demands in ways that lead to fuller and qualitatively better use of their limited time with the kids.

Each time Dick picks up his kids from school, for instance, he is struck by the freshness of the experience: the renewed joy of seeing his children running toward him, arms open wide, eyes shining, delighted to see him. He knows that he can't catch up on everything, and that if he can put aside his fussing about it, he and his kids will be off and running, enjoying their time together. The poignancy of each parting has eased somewhat over the years, not merely because of the passage of time, but because Dick has developed the confidence that he is an important part of his children's lives.

Much of his enjoyment of his children owes a lot to the way Dick schedules his time with them. Although each separation and divorce agreement is different from every other, we would like to share some ideas and suggestions for scheduling visits that have been helpful to us.

## Scheduling Visits

First of all, we think the occasional Saturday afternoon visit stinks. Kids need more time and so do we. If you haven't questioned the inadequacy of such an arrangement, please think again. If you find yourself saying, "Their mother won't allow me more time," we say, "Nuts!" Even if this skimpy schedule has all the trappings of legality, you probably can do better than that. Perhaps you're blaming your ex-wife rather than taking responsibility for your own laziness. But if you're not kidding us, maybe you need a better lawyer. One way or another let your kids know you want more time with them and try to make their mother understand how important it is. It will help if you have some ideas for other possible arrangements. We have a number of alternatives to offer, and although you may not feel you can manage all of them at the moment, they may help you to have an idea of what you can shoot for.

*Overnight visits:* The difficulties you discover when you first begin to have the kids stay overnight will simply tell you what you need to learn about caring for them. With a little preparation you'll probably find overnighters are a cinch. Later on in the book we'll have a few tips to make it still easier for you.

*The whole weekend:* If you find you can manage overnighters, why not graduate to the whole weekend or at least every other weekend? We've already seen that it takes some time really to relax and have a good time together, and when the kids leave afterward you may even feel glad to have a bit of peace and quiet. The satisfaction of a good long weekend with the kids will begin to replace the guilt and sadness that shorter visits encourage.

While you're at it, you might try picking them up on Friday after school and keeping them until Monday morning. That will really give you a complete weekend together. Then, if you want a Friday or Saturday night off once in a while, you can feel all right about getting a baby-sitter, because you'll still have two other evenings with them that weekend. We discuss other important advantages of this arrangement later on.

*One week night each week:* Having the kids one night a week, preferably overnight, will help you to keep in close touch with them and stave off the feeling of being strangers.

*Two week nights in a row* will permit you the additional experience of taking them to school in the morning and picking them up on the same day, giving you a complete, "normal" day with the kids, rather than just a piece of one. There's a nice feeling of continuity in doing this which you may miss otherwise.

If you put all of these combinations together, *you will actually have your children half of the time!* Say you decide to have them every other weekend (Friday to Monday) and Tuesday and Wednesdays—over a two-week period that adds up to seven days. It looks something like this:

M  Tu  W  Th  F  S  Su  M  Tu  W  Th  F  S  Su

This schedule includes not only every Tuesday and Wednesday night and every other Friday, Saturday, and Sunday night, it also includes Wednesday and Thursday morning and every other Monday morning. It may not seem like half the time because it is spread over a two-week period, but it is.

Lunch times aren't covered by this schedule on weekdays but sitters and lunch programs for school kids and day-care programs for preschoolers are a normal part of life for any working single parent.

*Lunch time:* Of course lunches with your kids are a particularly nice way of keeping in touch. David's kids can drop by for lunch with their dad very easily because he lives near their school and he has a job that's flexible enough to allow him to enjoy that time with his kids. Fathers with tighter work schedules can probably arrange to lunch at one of their children's favorite spots once in a while. Taking each of them separately to lunch may also be a good way of giving special attention to each of your children.

These are just some examples of arrangements which will allow you frequent and full enough contact with your children to dispel the short visit blues. But you may not be ready for this much contact yet. Many of us have to grow into it, becoming increasingly involved with our kids as we begin to feel the need and to see the possibilities for more time with our children. However, if you feel uncomfortable and unhappy about the amount of time you are currently spending with your kids, it's a good indication that you probably can do more and feel better.

If you're living too far away to see your kids frequently, none of this advice will seem pertinent. We'll have a few things to say later about the special problems of fathering at a distance. In the meantime, we are sorry if this discussion hurts, but we believe it may be important to alert you to possibilities you may have overlooked.

You may see yourself as helpless to do anything about fathering because *the kids* are so far away. But have you entertained the possibility of moving closer to them? We'd like you to reconsider your assumption that *you're* stuck because of your job, or owning a house, or other similar considerations. Kids are often regarded as less important than a father's employment, and men seldom conceive of themselves moving in order to be near their children. Neither of these assumptions necessarily has any validity and they may be worth reexamining if they are operating to keep you from your kids.

"Yeah, but what about my ex-wife?" you may demand. "She has a hand in all of this too, you know." We do know. You'll have to negotiate all of these problems and visiting arrangements with her (particularly if she has custody or there is joint custody). We hope that our later discussion pertaining to your relationship with your former wife will help you in your contacts and contracts with her. In the meantime, it's visits with the kids that are in focus. So let's talk some more about what those visits can be like.

## When Your Children Come for a "Visit"

For many legal, cultural, and practical reasons, separated fathers are faced with having their children as occasional "visitors." As we have seen, this fact has important and often frightening implications for the separated father, and particularly the newly separated father.

Some separation agreements provide for the kids visiting once a week or so, perhaps for an evening meal. Other agreements provide for times when the children can stay overnight at their father's home and still others include stipulations that permit the children to stay longer periods of time with their father—school vacations, a month in the summer, and so forth. Whatever the specific circumstances, separated fathers often feel that the limited amount of time they have with their children is precious and must be spent in ways specifically designed to ensure the maintenance of a loving relationship with their kids, and they fear that any miscues or inadequate planning will result in a damaging rift between themselves and their children. In short, they feel terribly vulnerable.

As a consequence, the newly separated father often spends an inordinate amount of time planning the children's visits, believing that these visits must be aesthetically and emotionally perfect if the children's love for him is to be maintained. He doesn't realize that his children want to see him every bit as much as he wants to see them, and that they probably don't have any great expectations about what they are going to do beyond the ordinary ones of spending time with a parent they love.

There are some kids, of course, who don't want to see their father, or who say they don't—kids who harbor real or imagined grievances against their father, who are sore about the separation itself, or who have been instructed in some way not to like their father for various reasons. There are also periods in children's development when they may need more attention from and contact with one parent or the other.

But most children need and want a good relationship with both of their parents even if they are temporarily confused by the emotional turmoil that invariably accompanies a separation. Once it is clear that they are not responsible for the separation and that they are not going to be abandoned, children quickly recover confidence in their relationship with their parents. In fact, they seem to recover much faster than their parents, and particularly their fathers. The separated father is most frequently the parent who is out in the cold, so to speak, without custody and having least contact with the children. As a consequence, he is usually the slowest to regain confidence in his relationship with the children.

Because of fear and uncertainty, and perhaps out of a sense of guilt, it is not unusual for the separated father to try orchestrating visits that go far beyond the expectations of any youngster. Kids don't expect to be wined and dined or taken to the movies every night. Like as not, they would rather relax and just enjoy being with their father. If wonderful and stimulating activities are the only things that they have to look forward to on visiting days, both father and children will be exhausted by their visits together. So special excursions and events should be kept special, just as they would have been if the father were living with his children all the time. The kids will like it better that way and so will their dad.

What's more, if each visit has to be an "emotional success," papa is destined to experience an awful lot of failures. For one thing, nobody can be that sweet and thoughtful all of the time, even if he wants to. We don't know of any father who doesn't get irritated with his kids sometimes, or who doesn't take his feelings out on them once in a while when he has an off day. The point is that it's normal to have fluctuations in mood that may "spoil" things occasionally.

But the newly separated father doesn't see it that way at first. He usually feels terrible if the visit with his children doesn't go as planned. Early in his separation, David was utterly heartbroken when his ugly mood "ruined" the FABULOUS WEDNESDAY EVENING DINNER with his boys. He saw it as a total disaster, because he knew he wouldn't see his kids again for days—not until their next visit—and this left him no opportunity to recover from the great disaster. He spent those days in self-incrimination and remorse. And his aggravation grew, because he knew that under "normal" circumstances, that is, if he and his kids lived together, such bad times would be corrected merely because he would see the children the next day when he was in a better mood.

Much to his amazement and relief David discovered that his kids still loved him the next week. And after a number of incidents of this sort over the years he realized that he didn't have to give up being a human being, whether he was nasty or nice at the moment, in order for his children to love and respect him. More than this, he found that being himself with his kids helped to free them to be themselves with him as well, unburdened of the unreasonable expectation that they had to be angels. When he and his kids have a fight now, David feels freer to acknowledge that his kids had some responsibility for the stuff hitting the fan. And even if it's his own irritability that brings on a fight, he no longer finds it necessary to saddle himself with guilt for his horrible intrusion into the otherwise cheerful lives of his innocent children.

It takes time for separated fathers to recover their perspective the way David did. Early in the process they tend to get bogged down by emotions which are based more on fantasy than reality. Already vulnerable because of feelings of failure that often accompany separation and divorce, separated fathers are particularly prone to feeling guilty and fearful about being a lousy parent. They may become terribly worried about their children's disapproval, including the possibility of being deserted by their kids. Even when these feelings have some basis in reality they may be greatly exaggerated, resulting in the father frightening himself unnecessarily. Whatever their cause, these feelings are compelling, and have far-reaching effects.

Our fears can get us into binds that may have profound effects on our relationships with our kids. One of the ways this may come about is by denying ourselves important things in the interests of being a "good" father, and then resenting the kids, feeling that they are somehow responsible for our loss. What happens, for example, if you have some work to do when the kids are scheduled to arrive, or if you've been wanting to fix a few things around the house and would like to get them done on a particular weekend? Is it really necessary to drop everything to spend the entire visit with your children? Perhaps you can. But if you feel resentful, or find yourself longing to fix the plumbing, or you're still thinking about washing the car, you and your kids may be better off if you go ahead and do it. You probably wouldn't have inhibited yourself if you were still living with them on a regular basis, so why stop yourself now?

The fact is you're probably spending more time actually interacting with your kids now than you did before you were separated, and there are limits to how selfless you can be at any given moment.

There will be times when you are full of energy and can give a lot, and other times when you need some energy input or some rest, or when you need to do your own thing as a human being. If your children happen to be with you at the times you really need something yourself and you attend to them instead, you may end up by getting into trouble with yourself, and with them as well. This kind of trouble may seem unavoidable if your children are very young and need more or less constant supervision. But other resources are usually available in the form of relatives and friends, and that lifesaver—baby-sitters. They can free you to do the things you want to do, before you go bonkers.

Some of the consequences of fatherly self-denial are subtle and some aren't. One of the more obvious is the wish that the kids would go away so that you could go about your business. Naturally, this leads to feelings of guilt. A more subtle consequence may ultimately affect the amount of contact you have with your children. You might be able to have your children at times other than those stipulated by your separation agreement, but you may not want them! You may only want to see them when you are "prepared" for them—when you are ready to give them all of your attention. And when you think about it, that's ridiculous. You may actually be reducing the time you could be with your children, and for what reason? Why shouldn't you and your children be together when you are each doing your own thing? Aren't there times when your kids find their own activities more interesting and important than yours? Do you think that they would find it strange if you felt the same way? And yet if you don't catch on to this notion you might actually end up avoiding your children.

Let's take a common example. There are times when your former wife might want to get away by herself and is unable to get a baby-sitter, or she might want to go away for an extended period of time but can't find anyone to care for the children. On such occasions, she might ask you to take them. If you are free to do what you want to do when your kids are with you, you will probably be free to welcome them at these unscheduled times. So, you'll get to see your children more frequently than you expected. You may even find yourself telling your ex-wife that you would be glad to have the kids more if she wants to get away. On the other hand, if your thinking runs along the line: "My God, if I have the kids this weekend I won't be able to do such and such, and I'm going to have to organize this and change that around [add your favorite curse words]"—you're going to resent their coming. And if you say that you "can't" have them when you really could, you'll feel guilty and defensive.

Of course, there will be times when you really can't take the kids, or when you just don't feel like being an instant baby-sitting service for your ex-wife. But these occasions are generally clear-cut. Saying "no" won't generate much guilt, unless, of course, you've been regularly refusing the kids even when it was reasonable for you to take them. Asking to have them over at another unscheduled time may help offset any bad feelings you may have about saying "no."

Denying yourself a normal life because the children are around can have a variety of negative consequences. But there are also very definite advantages for everyone concerned if they are with you while you go about your business as you normally would. One way, and a very important way that children learn about living and how to do all sorts of things is by seeing their parents in action. If your children see you cooking, fixing things, sewing, doing the wash, or filling out your income tax forms, they will begin to get some idea of how to do a number of things that they'll need to do when they become adults.

Even if they don't actively enter into the things you're doing, seeing you in action will serve as a model that will aid in their development. Because some of what you do as a separated father is identified as "woman's work" in our society, your children will learn broader roles for themselves than you probably did, sparing them much of the sexual chauvinism that is often part and parcel of child rearing in our society.

But don't get us wrong. We're not trying to say that your visits with your children are or should be anything but special. On the contrary, we know that the very circumstance of separation itself makes this limited time with your children very special—special because you have a chance to play your part, imparting values, knowledge, skills, and the like to your children—the way you would if you were living with them every day. They deserve the best, and we think the best is being yourself with them.

# 2. Relationships—

## The Social Context of Separate Fathering

Obviously, the process of becoming a separated father does not take place in a vacuum. It occurs in a social context, amid a variety of important relationships all having relevance and impact on the separated father and his children. The following section is devoted to some of the more important of these relationships.

Our main purpose in opening up these relations to discussion is to facilitate the father's constructive transition from the painful and often destructive interpersonal processes of separation to the enjoyment of co-operative and healthy relations in his new beginnings as a separated father.

We regret if in the process anything we say about these kinds of relationships is experienced as painful to people who may identify themselves with the various roles and especially if they feel themselves unsympathetically described. We are profoundly sorry if this is the case, because we know firsthand how painful these matters are to each person involved. But how else can we urge these individuals and fathers alike to more co-operative and harmonious relations with one another? For that is what we earnestly wish to do.

It is our hope that along with any embarrassment that may be occasioned by this kind of recognition, both fathers and other relevant parties will find in these discussions a sympathetic understanding of their predicaments with one another, and some hope for the future.

Naturally, we have made every effort to safeguard the privacy of the individuals upon whose experiences this book is based. The names—except for those of ourselves and our children—and the places mentioned in this book are fictitious. The incidents described, while based on actual events, are fictionalized presentations designed to illustrate problems encountered by many persons who have traveled these same bumpy roads toward separate fathering.

# Your Former Wife

It's safe to say that there aren't any easy separations. Even the "amicable" ones involve painful exchanges of feelings, and if the people involved are at all combative, the enmity can be almost overwhelming.

To people who have no need to see each other again, the rancor that usually accompanies separation might actually be beneficial, helping the couple dissolve their relationship. After all, it's probably easier to separate from someone who's attacking you than from someone who is loving and kind.

## A Relationship Persists

But for separated parents, it's another story. They still have to maintain some sort of relationship with one another in spite of their discomfort. While they may dissolve their marital bonds readily enough, they soon discover they're bound together through the children. This association goes far beyond casual contacts and simple civility. As you read through this book it will be obvious, if it isn't already apparent from your own experience, just how often the separated father must interact with his former wife.

Even if he doesn't see her every time he has to pick up the kids, he has to contact her to make adjustments in visiting times, or to discuss the logistics of transferring clothing and toys from one household to another. Every time he phones the children, his former wife may answer. He's likely to encounter her at parent-teacher meetings, school plays, sporting events, and the like. In short, she's ubiquitous. She shows up in any situation involving the children.

Yet sadly enough, even though a relationship with one's former wife is necessary, it's extremely difficult to maintain on a cordial level. There are a number of reasons for this difficulty beyond obvious differences in personality, lifestyle, and so on that may have initially led to the separation.

## In Spite of Pain

Since couples often have to make each other thoroughly miserable before they can part, the acrimony between them may reach appalling heights before they are willing to separate. When children are involved things may really have to get bad before they can part company. Parents often think they should stay together for "the sake of the children" or to avoid the shame and guilt of "abandoning" their kids.

As if this weren't bad enough, once the couple decides to separate or get a divorce, the legal system places them in an adversary position, a stance that both encourages and feeds into existing hostilities. In most places in North America, the legal process doesn't concern itself with what is best for everyone. Rather it requires that each "side" protect its own territory, fostering paranoia rather than cooperation. Wives are obliged to "get as much money as possible," while their husbands are encouraged to pay as little as they can. She attempts to control his visits with the children. He tries to make them as open-ended as possible, and on and on and on. . . .

So the irony of this situation is that after fighting it through and finally torturously dissolving their marriage, the former partners discover that they still have to maintain a relationship. Even those who manage to separate without hating each other balk at discovering that some important ties still exist. The unexpected intimacy of this relationship is a constant source of low-level irritation.

## Intimacy Persists

By intimacy we don't mean casual meetings at the theater or parties or other interactions that might occur because you have friends in common. Nor are we referring to chance encounters because you both live in a small town or even meetings to discuss matters concerning your children's welfare. Rather we are talking about a subtle, almost indefinable intimacy that occurs because you both have close bonds with your children, bonds which separation or divorce cannot eradicate. You are party to an intimacy that is experienced as gratuitous, unwanted, and awkward. And it's not a question of liking or despising your former wife that makes it so unnerving;

it's the lack of choice, the need constantly to go through her in order to have a relationship with your children.

It's also upsetting to discover that in playing her part as a co-parent your former wife has to have access to you too. These contacts may painfully remind you of old wounds you'd rather forget as well as confronting you with currently unresolved issues. Furthermore, she is not only intimately involved in your business together but becomes familiar with matters that aren't her business at all. Even though you may feel particularly vulnerable with her, she's privy to all sorts of information about you from finances to romances. And your lack of privacy results not merely out of direct contact with your ex-wife but in other ways as well.

## Children Increase Intimacy

Few people will know you more intimately than your children or give you away with greater innocence. They're all too willing to share little tidbits of information about one parent with the other.

Early in any visit with your kids, for example, you're likely to hear "Mommy this" or "Mommy that," and in the same way she's likely to hear about you. Whether they're funny or just boring, listening to these stories always seems to be at least somewhat annoying. Sometimes they are irritating reminders of your former wife, especially annoying because they compete with your time with the children, and at others they arouse jealous fantasies about good times with your children from which you've been excluded. Occasionally, these stories may really stir up trouble.

Unfortunately there are parents who betray their relationship with their children by using them directly or indirectly as spies or assault forces in a continuing war with their former spouses. But the kind of trouble we're talking about is more ordinary, usually inadvertent, yet thoroughly involving.

One agitated mother phoned the children's father shortly after the kids had returned to her place after spending the weekend with him and gave him hell for leaving the children alone "too long." He had run down to the corner store to get a carton of milk and may have been away all of ten minutes. Given the age and competence of the children, both parents could have agreed that this was a reasonable length of time for the children to be by themselves. But the children's conception of time had stretched their father's absence to an hour when they related the story to their mother. She was naturally anxious about her children's safety. He, in turn, was furious with her apparent lack of respect for his ability to care for the children without her supervision. Eventually these parents were able to sort out the difficulty and learned how to handle similar situations more amicably. Nonetheless, the painful confrontation did occur.

In this situation the kids might well have been aware that they were stirring up trouble by complaining. But in most instances, children probably haven't the slightest idea that they may be creating problems for their separated parents. In fact, more often than not it is the good things that happen to them with one parent or the other that kids like to share, erroneously assuming that everyone else will share their enthusiasm. These good things sometimes create as much trouble as the bad.

One of our clients recently bought a new house. One day, Charlie's two young daughters invited their mother to admire their rooms in their father's new house. Charlie's ex-wife not only saw the children's rooms, but took the opportunity to wander throughout the house taking note of new furnishings as well as old, prized possessions that were no longer hers. Finished with her tour, she couldn't help taking pot shots at Charlie before she left, hitting him with such subtleties as: "Gee, Charlie, I see you have a new stereo. That must have cost a bundle. I wish I had one." And, "What a nice blender. I've been thinking of getting one for years, but I just can't afford it." And, "I see you refinished your old kitchen table. It looks nice but I sure don't know why I let you take it when you left."

Positions were reversed for Charlie the following summer when his daughters proudly showed off the post cards their mother sent describing the grand old time she was having in the Far East. Since he was paying "child support" even though the children were staying with him for those two months, Charlie felt he was either paying for her trip, or making double support payments. Either way, he developed a lot of resentment out of a few post cards.

With their natural enthusiasm, children like Charlie's unwittingly play a significant and active part in maintaining the intimacy of the remaining relationship between their separated parents, sometimes, as we've seen, to the point where it hurts. Due to their open and ingenuous natures, kids can also be pretty direct in confronting you with a relationship with their mother. Kids often have an investment in getting you back together for their own particular reasons. Take the unique rationale Dick's son Robbie offered when he suggested enthusiastically, "You and Mom should get married, because you're great cooks!"

Although Dick appreciated the compliment to his cooking, both he and his new companion wondered about Robbie's logic and questioned the wisdom of his conclusion, as you might imagine. Robbie's actual reason for saying it illustrates the problem most separated children have in going from one parent to another, even when they have it "made" in both places. As Robbie put it, "When I'm with one of you I miss the other, and I just wish you'd get back together so I wouldn't feel that way."

## Others Remind You in Case You've Forgotten

In addition to your children, other people will reunite you as husband and wife without asking you about it at all. Acquaintances who don't know that you're separated may politely inquire about your wife's health. Tradespeople, salespersons, and others often assume that you're married because you have kids. As a result, you might have to field silly questions like, "And what will the little woman think?" which is bad enough when you're married but worse when you're a tender, newly separated father. One separated father, who had been living with a woman for a number of years, was asked by a moving man, "Will your wife like the television here?" He couldn't resist replying, "Yes, but my girl friend won't."

### Even Forms

Usually the joke isn't on the other person though. Being constantly reminded of your ex-wife by every government form, hotel registration, or credit application is draining as hell. Those anonymous twits who make up the forms seem to have some kind of voyeuristic need to know if you are married, separated, divorced, widowed, or just plain single. If marital status is really important, it seems to us that a simple "married-or-not" question ought to suffice.

We won't even go into what it must be like for your former wife, who is still stuck with your name!

## And Other "Interested" Parties

Worse still are those people who are perfectly aware of your marital situation, but who insist on asking you about your former wife anyway. Relatives and friends often make use of you as a source of information about her. They assume you're still in intimate contact with her and will know "How's she doing?" or "Is she happy, now?" and "Does she like her new place?"

Benign and genuinely interested as they might be, many people don't seem to realize that it might be painful for you to be linked so closely with your former spouse that you would actually be expected to know the latest news about her, or even her present state of mind. It seldom occurs to them that you might actually want to forget her and the pain associated with her, particularly in the early stages of separation. Besides, if they are really interested in her, why don't they ask *her* how she's doing? She might appreciate it.

We've found that when we've been exasperated enough to say this to people, these annoying questions are reduced. Relatives are another problem. We've found it almost impossible to keep them from being intrusive. However, we'll discuss relationships with them later.

## The Problems of Contact

Being reminded by others that you still have a relationship with your ex-wife may be painful to you, but actual contact with her is the real problem with which you have to deal. Contact is particularly difficult because anger generally plays such a big part when people separate. In addition to antagonisms fostered by the process, separation may also aggravate enduring personal animosities that may have characterized your marriage. Although separation may have brought relief from most of the acute conflicts of the marriage, the process of parting may create fresh wounds to add to the remaining pain and hostility. As if that isn't enough, the uncertainties and imbalances which inevitably occur in the early postseparation period, also bring their own problems and conflicts. It's certainly an awkward base on which to found an effective relationship as separated parents.

Normally, when we deal with relationship problems, we try to work with both parties involved. For obvious reasons, this is often difficult to do with separated couples. But we've discovered a number of things that separated fathers can do to facilitate the process of achieving a co-operative relationship with their former wives. The first task is to re-establish sufficient emotional balance to allow you to be in contact with your ex-wife. Your next task is to ascertain the amount of contact that is actually necessary or desirable. There are guidelines to help you accomplish these and other tasks that can improve the quality of your contacts, and hence the quality of your parenting.

## Anger

Much of the emotional imbalance experienced at the time of separation is a function of anger. While anger might facilitate separation it also contributes to the discomfort of your interactions with your ex-wife and makes necessary co-operation difficult. Other emotions may impede co-operative relations, but most of these feelings find expression through anger as well. This doesn't mean that you have to be a helpless victim of anger. There are ways of coping with its potentially disastrous effects, and there are even times when it may actually serve some useful function.

## Anger Can Be Useful

Sometimes it may be better to express your anger when you feel something is wrong than tacitly accept a situation that is unsatisfactory. Under these circumstances your anger may serve as a useful tool for communicating loudly and clearly when someone has difficulty understanding the meaning behind your words. A furious outburst may finally convince your former wife that you really want the kids, for example, overcoming her utter disbelief.

When Jennifer and Marvin were preparing to separate, Marvin spent several therapy sessions bemoaning his potential loss of the children. Jennifer obviously didn't believe him. She had trouble seeing him as genuinely interested in the children. Her persistent expression of disbelief finally triggered an uncharacteristically violent display of anger as Marvin screamed at her in frustration, tears of rage streaking his face as he stormed out of the room. Jennifer was astonished. She began to realize that her husband was serious about wanting the children.

In a similar situation, another client refused to believe her husband could handle the job of caring for the children, let alone enjoy it. His fathering, which had always been lax, had become almost nonexistent during the weeks prior to separation. It took a display of anguished fury on his part to allow her to see that he was not an indifferent father.

Both of these wives were surprised by their husband's investment in their children, and genuinely relieved to discover that their husbands wanted to share responsibility for raising them after separation. In these instances, anger happened to be helpful in communicating things that were not being heard.

## The Pointing Finger

Anger may help to get someone's attention sometimes, but more often it chases away the very people with whom you need contact. Furthermore, to the surprise of the participants, anger frequently turns out to be a disguised way of asking for something.

We've noticed when working with couples that when one of them seems to be figuratively pointing a finger at the other, the pointee often ducks, much to the surprise and annoyance of the pointer. We may then ask the accuser actually to *point* a finger at the other person, gradually rotating and opening the hand until it is palm up, thus changing an aggressive posture into a supplicant one. Try it. This experiment reveals to both parties the fact that their accusations often conceal their need for something. It also explains the reason for an aggressive cover. An open palm feels distinctly vulnerable in contrast to a pointing finger. In other words, it may be a lot easier to ask for things with anger, even though it drives the other away, because being safe overrides being effective in getting what you need.

## Knowing Your Anger

If you aren't ready for the open palm approach, you probably still aren't finished with your anger. But you can certainly become more effective as a father in the postseparation relationship if you are able to exercise some control of your emotions. Before you can have any choice in the matter, however, you have to have an awareness of your feelings. People often walk around without knowing they are angry about something. Irritability or a puzzling, low-level depression may be your only indication.

Sometimes only the feeling of anger is evident. You may feel "inexplicably" infuriated by your ex-wife. Instead of inquiring into the feelings further, you may try to hide the anger from yourself and others, embarrassed by your supposed irrationality or weakness in getting "stirred up over nothing." As a consequence you may end up exploding inappropriately at other people, including your children.

When he went to pick up the kids, Bob left his ex-wife's house inexplicably furious with her, and later complained in his sessions with us how grumpy and nasty he'd been afterwards with his kids. Exploring the situation further we discovered that his ex-wife had asked him some questions about filling out her income tax form. Bob began to recognize that this relatively innocuous request had made him furious. He had been too embarrassed to say anything about it at the time because he felt that his anger was inappropriate, but it ended up spilling over anyway with his children.

Bob realized that his anger had originated in the feeling that his wife was still relying on him in much the same way she had during their marriage. What had been merely irritating then was intolerable to him after separation.

Once he appreciated the cause of his anger, he was better able to accept it. It made some sense to him. In this particular case, Bob was able to go a few steps further. He recognized that his former wife might well feel lost doing her tax computations, because during their marriage he had always done it. At the same time, he was able to acknowledge and accept the fact that it wasn't his job any longer and that he didn't need to feel guilty (hence angry) about not wanting to help her.

## Owning Your Anger

Knowing the reasons for your feelings, and validating them so you don't experience them as irrational, may help a great deal, as we've seen in Bob's case. But it's important to remember that even though your anger may be stimulated by your former wife, that doesn't mean that she is to blame for your feelings. Holding her responsible for your anger would be both silly and misleading.

Your anger and all the rest of your feelings *belong to you,* and how you respond to your ex-wife (or anybody else for that matter) is your own business. Look at it this way. If we said, "She put anger into me," we'd sound foolish, yet we imply just that sort of thing when we talk about someone "making" us angry. A more accurate description of what actually happens might be something like, "When I'm around my ex-wife, I make myself angry."

The distinction is extremely important because one view leads to a kind of blind, helpless reactivity to other people while the other opens you to change. Blaming someone else for the way you're feeling implies that she or he controls you. You'd be in serious trouble if that were actually true. On the other hand, taking responsibility for your own emotional responses, and thus "owning" them, allows you to have a choice in the way you act. You are in your own hands and not controlled by someone else.

## Your First Response Needn't Be Your Last

Most of us need some practice in developing a larger repertoire of responses to our experiences. Your first reaction to frustration in dealing with your former wife will probably be anger or resentment, but because it is your first response doesn't mean that it's the only response available. You don't have to be stuck with it just because it was the first in line. Your initial reactions may be so compelling as to convince you that you can't help but feel the way you do. As long as you remain convinced that this is the case, other responses will seem impossible. Furthermore, you may be so addicted to your favorite way of responding to your ex-wife, that you are reluctant to let go of it even when you realize it's under your control.

People can sometimes be therapeutically tricked into experiencing feelings they think unavailable to them. Take Jack, for instance. He came to us feeling extremely "depressed." He was a complete failure. Not only had his marriage gone to pot, but he was sure his kids hated him, and why shouldn't they, and so on. As therapists, we just couldn't take Jack's depression seriously, though we never doubted for a minute that he felt depressed. It was obvious to us, from all the other things that he told us, that he was a competent person more than capable of handling his life, and that he actually had a close and affectionate relationship with his kids. As the session progressed, Jack became more and more angry with us. We weren't taking his depression seriously enough or treating him the way we were "supposed" to. Nor were we properly chastened when he mentioned it. Then, in the midst of his indignation he started to laugh. It had suddenly dawned on him as he shouted about being ill-treated and depressed that there was nothing depressed about him. He was actually angry. Awareness of how he'd been tricked out of depression simultaneously released Jack from his outraged anger, allowing him to laugh at himself.

Jack was exhilarated. Freed from the emotions with which he had bound himself, he felt hope for the future. Even though he knew that he would probably again revert to his usual way of reacting, he felt his added awareness gave him some chance to break the pattern.

## Taking Control of Yourself

If other people can help you shift from one way of feeling to another, it's clear that change is possible. It's also clear that you needn't be stuck with your feelings, however compelling they may be. But most of the time a therapist or counselor isn't handy when things get rough. You have to help yourself in some way.

In the long run, you may be able to look at things in a different way so that personal attacks evoke feelings like curiosity rather than anger. But for the moment, you'll have to devise short term ways of coping with strong emotions.

There are a number of things you can do to get control of yourself and your situation, and none of them require composure or saintliness. Even if you are red-faced and furious you can act in your own behalf. For example, you can keep your mouth shut and walk away, or you can say that you'll call back later and hang up. In other words, if the situation triggers feelings you can't handle well, leave.

A corollary to this prescription is to act only when you are ready. Act when you're on good terms with yourself, when you're in a "good space" and not before. If you become angry with your ex-wife, leave and blow off steam somewhere else in a way that doesn't do yourself or others harm.

You can beat up a cushion, or strangle a pillow, or you can yell your head off, preferably where no one else can hear you. Try really letting go of yourself in a place where it's safe to do so. Get into it and exaggerate every emotion, accusation, and complaint until you begin to hear how ridiculous and funny you sound. When you can laugh at yourself again, then you'll know you're ready to act.

Incidentally, when you have that head of steam up you needn't waste all that wonderful energy on a mere pillow. Some of it can be channeled into constructive activity. Cleaning house, washing the car, pounding nails, and the like, can be done with incredible speed when energized by anger.

Some people find it more helpful to talk. Complaining to their therapist, minister, or goldfish helps them to let go of anger before they return to the issue. Charlie, for example, the father who had suffered in silence during his ex-wife's inspection of his new home, phoned a friend the minute she left. His friend soon had him laughing again about the whole thing, having confirmed the legitimacy of Charlie's anger.

Instead of making a scene when his former wife threatened to prevent him from seeing his children, another separated father turned to his lawyer for help. The lawyer made a few phone calls and arranged for the father to pick up the kids.

Both of these separated fathers successfully avoided prolonged and unproductive hassles with their former spouses by talking to another person.

## Separating Yourself from Her Anger

But what do you do when it isn't you but your former wife who is furious? When you're struck forceably with the realization that she hasn't read our section on self-control, and she's bouncing every insult and threat off your skull she can think of, what do you do? We suggest that you duck. Walk away, and don't worry about your dignity. Taking a beating won't do either of you any good. Remember that you still control your own legs. Use them.

It's only fair to warn you, of course, that this may make her mad as hell. Unless she's actually relieved to see you go, we can guarantee your little stroll will annoy her further, especially if she thinks that you "have to" remain in the situation to work it out, i.e., take your punishment. Remember, this demand that you stay is only a ploy invented by aggressors to persuade gullible victims to remain in the open. We used to call it being "chicken" when you walked away from a fight. Here, we call it smart. Don't be dumb enough to think you have to hang in there if you really don't want to.

Although your former wife may become angrier when you walk away, getting her mad is not the point of this exercise. Good communication and good health is the idea. If you end up hanging around taking a pounding, you'll be doing yourself a disservice. And if you keep that sort of thing up you may be in serious trouble with yourself (hello depression, hiya ulcer, how's the old blood pressure?).

Aside from doing yourself harm, you probably won't improve communication with your ex-wife. You're likely to end up reacting to her anger with your own, bringing us right back to where we started. So take a walk. Leaving is certainly one of the privileges of separation. You might as well take advantage of it.

## Absent Without Leaving

Some people don't need to walk away in order to depart. They're adept at side-stepping the impact of a zapping (*olé*) when they have no idea what's behind their former wives' fury, or have little hope of finding out.

A friend of ours decided that every time his wife phoned to dump garbage on him, in the absence of further information from her, he might as well attribute the attacks to something other than himself. Perhaps she was having trouble with her current boyfriend, or the kids were getting on her nerves. Maybe it was the barometric pressure. Who knew? Whether his diagnosis was correct or not didn't matter. By providing himself with a reason for his ex-wife's aggressiveness, one that had nothing to do with himself, he substantially reduced demands on himself to respond with an attack of his own.

## Going with the Blow

Another judo-like move is to go with the blow rather than to parry or counterattack. If you accept outwardly what your former wife says about you as true for her, without accepting it at all for yourself, both you and she may find some satisfaction. "Yeah, you're absolutely right," you might say. "I am a bastard. And what's more I lie a lot, too. Let's face it. I'm a selfish pig, and you probably shouldn't even waste your time talking to me." If you exaggerate the self-accusations it usually sounds so silly that even your ex-wife may end up laughing. At least she'll have something to think about later. There may be enough satisfaction in just hearing you acknowledge culpability, even if you're being facetious, for her to lay off for a while. And there may be something in it later for you, too. In the meantime passive "acceptance" may give you a breather, a partial escape that allows you to finish whatever business you may have with your ex-wife.

## But Stay Tuned In

Just as your own anger may sometimes have constructive purposes, your wife's antagonism may represent a frustrated attempt to communicate something important that you are having trouble hearing. The quicker you hear it, the sooner she'll lay off. While you are doing some of the fancy footwork we've described to stave off her blows, keep part of you tuned to the distress frequency. Even if you can't translate the message yourself, knowing that something important may be hidden by the static will allow you to find a translator, a friend or counselor who may be able to help you understand what your ex-wife is trying to tell you.

By the same token, if you've been trying unsuccessfully to express a message of your own that she doesn't seem able to listen to, we suggest that you ask her to consult with someone else she feels she can trust to check out what you're saying. Referring her to other people is not only an offer of good faith and trust on your part, it's also a graceful way of terminating an interview that has reached an impasse without throwing a tantrum.

## Apologize When You Blow It

Now, if in spite of all this good advice you explode at your former wife and really let her have it, the situation is still recoverable. After you've calmed down, and you've given your self-righteousness a rest, you may be able to begin taking a look at yourself.

Most of us aren't happy with ourselves when we go overboard in an argument. We feel uncomfortable remembering what we've said. Our own real (rather than advertised) motives begin to sift through, and we may regret that they weren't better expressed. Genuinely sorry about our own behavior, we can say so.

Following one of these blowups, one guy we know felt terribly restless about the angry exchange he had had with his ex-wife. He prowled around his apartment with the angry scene still in his head, arguing bitterly with her. Dimly at first, something about his actions began to feel unpleasantly familiar. He was appalled when he suddenly realized that he had fallen back into the old pattern of fighting with his wife, a pattern at once futile and depressing. He wanted no more of that useless turmoil. What he wanted was peace. He also began to worry about how the scene might affect his seeing the kids that weekend. Being "right" or "winning" suddenly seemed to matter less to him than it had at the time of the fight. Tired of wandering around the apartment worrying, he telephoned his ex-wife and apologized for having blown up.

He didn't know how she would react. All he knew was that he felt badly about how he had behaved and wanted to communicate his renewed good will and his willingness to listen to her. As it turned out, she was herself contrite about the fight and pleased with the opportunity to make amends. Within two hours of their battle these two people had re-established a co-operative working relationship. Our friend was so pleased with himself and the outcome he wondered why he hadn't thought of apologizing before in these situations.

## Making the Best of It

Perhaps it's expecting a great deal of people who are separated to suggest that they put on their best manners for each other. We know it's like asking for the moon in some cases. Linda and Harry, for example, who had despised each other for years found even ordinary civility not only impossible but intolerable for them. The antipathy between them was so great when they first separated that the only way they were able to talk to each other at all was through their lawyers. And then, rather than trying to negotiate even the simplest disagreements, each would try to force the other to capitulate. But even Harry and Linda had to let go of their expensive legal go-betweens and their dog fights as they began to appreciate the necessity for co-operative parenting in the interests of their children. It also took too much energy and money the other way, so they began to talk to each other a little more sensibly.

Even if you don't feel very nice about your former wife, or she about you, we'd like to suggest some ways to help you keep your nose clean, to avoid unnecessary trouble and, we hope, to make the best of the co-parenting relationship with your former wife.

## Reducing Contact

One of the most obvious ways of reducing some of the strain in your relationship with your former wife is to reduce the amount of contact you have with her. A trip to the Fiji Islands would certainly reduce a lot of the stress, wouldn't it? However difficult things were, you'd sure feel a lot better there than hanging around. Obviously that's not what we mean. Assuming you want to be with your kids rather than their mother, we suggest you find ways to see less of her and more of them.

If you usually pick up the kids at their mother's place, it means you probably have to see her as well. That can be awkward at times, and even painful if either of you use these occasions to stir up conflicts. It's often difficult to resist taking cheap shots, or bringing up unfinished business. So, if either of you are prone to do this, we suggest that you pick the kids up at school, the day-care center, nursery, or baby-sitter's rather than at her place. If you can keep them overnight or for an entire weekend and return them directly to school, nursery, or sitter yourself, you will not only eliminate any chance of conflict, but you'll also enjoy the process itself, and start off your time with the children in a better space.

Their mother may telephone at first to see if you picked the kids up on time and to make sure that they are safe. While you may read into this an implication that you are irresponsible, take it easy. You may feel a little edgy and "unfinished" yourself leaving the kids off at school and not picking them up the same night. You may feel as if you've misplaced them somewhere or forgotten to pick them up, even though you know they are supposed to go to their mother's after school. In fact, you might even be the one calling *her* to have a reassuring word with the kids.

Of course, if your children are old enough and are able to get to your place themselves, as David's are now, that's even better. Then they can drop by any time they want. On the other hand, there is really no help for contact with their mother if your kids are too young to go to school or don't have a sitter. You'll just have to have patience. They'll be in school soon enough.

## Guidelines for Picking Up the Kids

There are times when picking up the kids at their mother's is unavoidable regardless of how old they are. Birthdays and holidays or other special occasions won't always fall neatly at "your" times on the visiting schedule, and of course you'll have to pick them up at their mother's during the summer and other times when school is out. A few guidelines might help make these necessary contacts a bit more pleasant.

Picking-up time is time to be with your kids rather than time for you and your former wife to discuss business, especially dirty business. If something needs to be resolved, make an appointment with your ex-wife. Doing so will acknowledge the problem and will also make it clear that picking-up time isn't the right time to do it. If a few words will bring you up to date on the children, fine. But try to keep things as pleasant as you can, even if you have to fake it a little. If you allow yourself to get upset, you'll only foul up your time with the kids.

If your ex-wife hangs around too long when she drops them off at your place, or you find it uncomfortable to have her there at all, make the effort to pick them up yourself. It is usually easier for you to leave her place gracefully than it is to ease your former wife out your own door. You have a lot more control over your own behavior than you do over hers.

## Structure Helps

The more routine your visiting arrangements are the less you will need to see the children's mother. So, make clear-cut arrangements for picking up the children, and stick to them. Make any necessary changes *ahead* of time. Just as you would appreciate consideration from your ex-wife on this score, try to respect her right to make plans for the times when she doesn't have the kids. Don't go changing your mind at the last minute unless it's unavoidable, or unless you want trouble.

Even though you may need things open-ended when you first separate, visiting arrangements should be structured as soon as possible. This will eliminate uncertainty for everyone, and allow your children to know when they are going to see you. In addition, making a firm commitment will re-establish your sense of responsibility and closeness to your children.

## Be a Good Co-parent

Be a good co-parent. Since you're still in partnership in raising the children, be the best partner you can. Act in good faith and with respect for your former wife. Try not to comment negatively on her behavior no matter what you think of her or how angry you are at the moment. This is particularly important around your children. Chopping up their mother could evoke divided loyalties, so spare the children from feeling like ping-pong balls by showing some restraint. If you have to gripe about your ex-wife, and there's no doubt there will be occasions when you'll feel as if you'll explode unless you do, talk it over with your friends or professional confidants privately.

It'll help you to unload your aggravation and regain perspective without creating more problems for yourself in the process.

On a more positive note, we'd like to go even further by recommending that you support the children's mother whenever possible. Though you may differ with her as to her attitudes and behavior vis-à-vis the children (and what's more natural than differences?), keep in mind that she's probably doing the best job she can under the circumstances. It's fine to let your kids know that you have a different point of view on some of these issues, but you can also make it clear that you respect their mother's position, supporting rather than undermining her as a parent.

We're not suggesting that you support behavior or attitudes you feel will be detrimental to your kids. Adults aren't infallible and children need respect and validation as people. When you have a choice between supporting an erring adult or confirming reality for your child, we think authority has to come last. But keep an eye on your own prejudices when deciding tight calls in these situations. Any sense of righteousness or pleasure at the other parent's expense is a sure cue it's time for restraint on your part. Remember, your former wife will be making these same decisions about you.

## When She Isn't

No doubt sometimes you'll wish your former wife would extend to you the same good faith and respect we've asked you to show her. Ex-wives don't always do so. This is not always motivated by hostility, although it may be difficult for you to see otherwise while you're under siege.

Perhaps the most shortsighted thing separated mothers do is question the competence of their former husbands to care for the children. It's easy for separated fathers to get defensive as hell about this kind of indictment, because they may feel their right to see the children is being threatened. Newly separated fathers in particular are especially vulnerable to this kind of criticism, since some accusations of paternal incompetence are usually true to a degree. Because "mothering" hasn't been their job up to the time of separation, they often lack adequate preparation for assuming full child-care responsibilities. They need some encouragement while they're going about learning to take care of the children, not criticism. But, separation isn't an easy time for separated mothers, and frustration and anxiety over their own problems may surface in criticism about their former husbands' competence as parents.

Even if they seem more like accusations than anything else, one way of dealing with questions about your fathering is to acknowledge areas where you're having difficulty and to invite advice about handling problem situations. Because you're learning, any tips your former wife may offer, or problems she may bring to your attention, will be very helpful, even if they don't seem to be offered with help in mind.

If you are able to listen undefensively, you may begin to see some of the reasons behind your ex-wife's "insinuations," including, of course, some of your genuine mistakes. She may be feeling very uneasy, for example, about not having control over the kids when they are at your place. It may be very easy for you to identify with these feelings. Most parents get nervous when control is out of their hands, at least until they've been reassured that it's safe to share responsibility with the school system, the day-care center, or whoever is taking care of the kids.

The children's mother may also experience some of the same grief and anger that you may feel in losing input into the children's lives as a result of separation. She may miss them when they aren't "home." Her release from child-care duties when the children are with you may also bring on feelings of guilt, especially if she finds herself enjoying her freedom from the kids, just as the increased responsibility may bring you frustration as well as joy.

Clearly, there's a great deal more involved in these questions than your actual competence to take care of your children. So, although you need to maintain your right as a separated father to care for your kids in your own particular way, it's wise to recognize and respect any anxiety or discomfort the children's mother may be having, even if she doesn't seem to extend you the same courtesy. She needs time to learn, too.


## Good Communication

Many of the interactions we've described between the children's parents have involved either rancor and suspicion, or at best one-sided expressions of good will. While this may faithfully reflect the emotional highlights of the relationship between people who have recently separated on the whole it isn't a fair representation of the day-to-day, week-to-week interactions between separated persons with kids. Their interactions are really more ordinary, concerned as they are with the everyday task of raising children.

Personal quarrels have to be set aside sufficiently for you to co-operate with each other in the task of caring for your kids. Good communication is necessary, and the better the communication is, the easier it will be for you and your children.

## Good Parenting

Exchanges of information about the children are very important to bridge the gap between visits, especially when the kids are too young to tell their folks what's going on. Parents must depend on each other to keep up to date on the kids, to make one another aware of special events, and to find out about changes that are taking place in the lives of their children.

It's nice to keep up on the latest developments so you can be prepared to encourage them. If one of you discovers an effective way of toilet training your toddler that seems to be working well, informing the other parent can assure a continuity and consistency that will help your son or daughter enjoy a rapid transition from "baby" to "little kid."

Sharing information, ideas, and even some of the techniques and philosophy of child rearing can help both of you to evolve the best way of raising your children under your particular circumstances, facilitating rather than impeding their development and growth.

Everyone benefits from this kind of co-operation. You and your ex-wife will have less work to do for one thing, if both of you consistently support the children in learning everyday skills like tying shoelaces, washing dishes, and making their beds. Besides other practical advantages, there's a lot of satisfaction in seeing children becoming self-sufficient and enjoying new-found talents and skills.

Intellectual abilities can be encouraged in meaningful ways through timely exchanges of information about what the children are learning at the moment. One parent may notice a particular kind of book or puzzle that has captured a child's interest, for instance, sending it along on the next visit.

It's worth mentioning that separated parents also have to rely on bits and pieces of information from their kids to find out how their children are doing. Exchanges of information about the children's perceptions are very helpful for getting a better picture of what's going on. For example, you may see that your kid is doing okay as far as her report card is concerned, but discover that she's unhappy with school because she feels she's being picked on by one of the teachers. Consultation with her mother may reveal other reasons your daughter neglected to mention to you which may help both of you to understand and decide how best to help your daughter.

Health care is another area of enormous importance, which demands good communication. Both you and your former wife need to be kept current about the children's state of health. Perhaps you don't need to know about every cold or bruised knee they've had, but if one of your kids is running a fever or has some special health problem you'll want to be informed about it. And if one of your children has to see a doctor while he's with you, you'll need to let his mother know all the details, including his reactions to the treatment, so she's properly prepared to deal with it on his return.

Illnesses don't follow anyone's visiting schedule so patience and consideration for the other parent's concerns and problems in caring for the children are very important. If the kids are too sick to come to your place or they're too ill to return to their mother's after a visit, arrangements need to be made to cope with the situation, allowing for the special stresses it creates for everyone.

So whatever the issue, whether it is health care or learning, day care or music lessons, good communication between you and the children's mother will assure your kids the kind of parenting they need.

# Your Parents

Because your parents are also the grandparents of your children, they may feel they have a special and important involvement in your separation. For this and other reasons their response to your separation may be motivated by their own needs as well as by concern for your well-being and the well-being of your children.

## Taking Your Separation Personally

Some parents certainly take separation personally. "How can you do this to me?" one guy's mother demanded when her son announced his separation. In such instances, it's hard to know exactly what kind of personal investment your parents have in your marriage that makes the news of separation so upsetting. You can only try to read between the lines attempting to guess what's really bothering your parents.

## Reflections on Their Own Marriage

One possibility is that your parents may be reacting to your separation from the perspective of their own marriage, like many of your friends and acquaintances. They may become defensive about the marvels of matrimony, even going so far as trying to patch things up. Or they may blame you for behaving badly, for not standing by your wife and kids the way you "should" have.

Dissatisfaction with their own marital roles may appear undisguised, reflecting their personal prejudices about marriage. One or the other of them may congratulate you, for instance, on "finally" getting out of "that" marriage, and either of them may take the opportunity to express personal resentment toward your former wife.

## Conflicts of Interest

Whatever their reaction, there is no question that your parents will probably feel torn by their competing relationships with you, your children, and your ex-wife, not knowing exactly what to do, having their own peculiar sympathies and biases, and wanting to protect their own interests as well.

A mother distressed by her son's pain might also dislike his leaving his wife, wondering to herself or her son, "Why couldn't you stay together like your father and me?" One or both may become irritated or withdraw, uncertain how to resolve their own ambivalent feelings or practical conflicts. "What do we do about Judith now? We invited you all to the cottage next month. Are you coming with the kids, or is she, or what?"

Guilt about their own shortcomings as models may emerge in the form of depression or withdrawal, irrelevant apologies or hostility, making you wonder what on earth is going on with them.

Some parents may resent your making a "mess" of your life, involving them in unwanted parental roles all over again. As a result, they may want as little to do with you as possible. They usually simmer down when their fears about you or your kids moving in with them, or otherwise burdening them financially, fail to materialize. They may even begin to show an interest in you and your children again when they realize you're not going to inundate them with your needs.

## Supportive Parents

In contrast, other parents are supportive right from the start. They have enough insight to know that you, your former wife, and your children are going through a difficult and traumatic time. These parents tend to provide both practical and emotional support during the worst stages of separation.

The parents of one of our clients insisted that he and his children fly to Florida for a couple of weeks' vacation at their expense. Other parents have offered their services as baby-sitters for the grandchildren, sometimes for long periods of time, giving their sons and daughters-in-law the room to adjust to the separation. And some out-of-towners have even had their grandchildren come to live with them for several months while the separating couple got settled.

Most parents probably aren't able to be quite so magnanimous, but many come through with an understanding phone call or a sympathetic letter when it's really needed, cutting through the isolation and loneliness of separation. Dick's folks, half a continent away, called him long distance just to let him know they were thinking of him, and were aware of the difficult time he and his family were going through.

While some parents respond with almost intuitive understanding during the crisis of separation, there are other parents who don't have a clue about what is really going on, and are too embarrassed to ask, and sometimes they may be paralyzed by conflicting loyalties. For whatever reason, these parents behave as if nothing has happened, avoiding mention of your separation or discussion of your future plans as a separated person and father.

If this happens, you will have to take the initiative, clueing them in on what's happening, and you'll have to let them know if there is anything they can do to help. You might have to invite yourself over for dinner perhaps, and single-mindedly bring up the topic of separation. Since your parents will have it on their minds anyway, bringing it up will be doing them a favor. Many of these slow-footed parents can be surprisingly responsive and helpful when they've been brought up to date and given some guidelines for responding to your separation.

## Parents as Grandparents

For some parents of separated fathers, it is their role as grandparents that leaps to the forefront, overshadowing any other role or consideration. If their grandchildren are especially precious to them, the threat of separation may be as keen as your own, and considering the fact that the rights of grandparents are rarely considered at all in divorce, their alarm is understandable. As a consequence, news of your separation may activate a variety of emotional reactions, including anger and rejection. This was true in Ian's case.

## Grandma Jekyll and Grandpa Hyde

Ian lived in Flagstaff, Arizona, at the time of his separation. On hearing the news of the separation, Ian's parents flew from California to be with their grandchildren, carefully picking a time when the children would be with Ian's wife, Cynthia. Without letting Ian know about it, they arranged to stay with Cynthia, refusing even to see Ian when he discovered they were in town.

For Ian's parents, the relationship with their grandchildren was paramount. They were shocked and furious with Ian for "leaving his family." They felt that he should have stayed with Cynthia for the "sake of the children," and, although they would never say it, for their own convenience. It had been far less complicated for them to be grandparents to their grandchildren when the family had been intact. They were annoyed in the extreme to find themselves in the midst of the confusion and inconvenience of a "broken home."

After the separation, Ian's parents felt that they had to maintain their relationship with their grandchildren at all costs. Since Cynthia had custody of the children, Ian's parents were prepared to abandon Ian. They believed that they should keep the lines of communication open with Cynthia to assure them easy access to the grandchildren, and they figured, on the basis of some rather convoluted reasoning, that the best way to do this would be to jettison their lines of communication with Ian, disassociating themselves from him completely.

Ian tried desperately to alter the situation. He called his parents long distance and wrote many letters, some pleading, some very angry. He tried to explain the reasons for his separation and told his parents that he needed their support. But they refused to respond.

Finally, Ian handled the situation in the only way that seemed open to him. Just as he had mourned the loss of his own family, he began the process of mourning the loss of his parents. Giving up hope of reconciliation, he permitted himself to grieve. After a period of mourning he was able to get back to his own life, returning to it with renewed energy, because he no longer felt that he had to expend himself in fruitless attempts to win back his parents.

Oddly enough, this particular story has a relatively happy ending. Ian's parents found out that Ian and his children were coming to California to visit some friends. They called him at the friend's house

and asked him to come to see them with the kids. Although under-
standably reluctant to get involved once again with his parents, Ian
was unable to turn down the invitation. The afternoon was pleasant,
and eventually he and his parents re-established a fairly good relationship.

In spite of the reconciliation, Ian was still a bit bitter, particularly
since his parents never apologized for what they had done, nor acknowledged their part in the temporary estrangement. Nonetheless,
Ian was happy about regaining a relationship with his parents, and
pleased that his parents had not only acknowledged the importance
of Ian's relationship with his kids, but had recognized, albeit with
surprise, what a good father their son was.

## Grandparents and Your Role as a Separated Father

Most parents won't go as overboard as Ian's, wooing their
daughter-in-law at their own son's expense. But like Ian's, your folks
will probably have a blind spot about your role with the children following separation. Your mother and father will probably assume,
like everyone else, that your former wife will be raising the children,
while their conception of your role in the family becomes hazy at
best.

Almost every grandparent will have to be educated about what
your new role will be as a separated father. You'll have to define
things very concretely for them, that is, as soon as it becomes clear to
you what you're doing.

It took a lot more than hints, for example, to persuade one set of
grandparents to mail the children's birthday and Christmas gifts to
their son's place rather than to their former daughter-in-law's. It just
hadn't occurred to them that their grandchildren lived with their son
part of the time, and celebrated special occasions with him as well as
with their mother. Once they got the picture, the correspondence for
the kids really picked up, to their delight as well as their dad's.

It's nice for you when your parents understand and acknowledge
your role as a father. It is also important to them, because their own
right to see their grandchildren is made uncertain by separation.
Knowing that you will continue to have a vital role as a parent will

help to reassure them of the security of their own relationship with their grandchildren.

It must also be said that your children have a similar right to know their grandparents on both sides, not only because of the goodies for which Grandma and Grandpa may be famous, but because it's nice for people to know where they come from, to have some sense of their own history and identity. On the whole, it's a good thing if both sets of grandparents are treated with consideration and respect by both you and your former wife. Any support grandparents can provide your children will be welcome, and a good relationship between kids and their grandparents, filled as it generally is with love and indulgence, is something to be prized always.

## Your Parents and You

Parents may play any of the roles we've talked about, or do any of the helpful or crazy things we've described, because they, too, are complex human beings. Whether we end up revering them as models or making them negative examples for our own parenting, our parents, living or not, continue to be important in our lives.

Separation may occasion a widening of an already existing "generation gap" between you and your parents, dusting off such one-liners as: "You're just being self-indulgent by getting divorced." Or, "You kids think you can just walk out when things get tough." On the other hand, you may find your separation brings out the best and most human qualities in your parents, narrowing the distance between you.

Under the special circumstances of separation and divorce, parents may share intimate secrets about their own relationship. They may reveal doubts and indecisions about their marriage, making a loving gift of their own humanity, touching you as a fellow human being and sealing the bonds between you with compassionate understanding.

Witness one mother and father seeking to comfort their recently separated son. "We almost separated when you were very young, son," his father began. "We were very unhappy together. But we couldn't do it, because of the depression, and then the war came along and your sister was born. We sometimes think we should have separated anyway, in spite of the difficulties. We are glad there aren't the same obstacles for you two." And his wife added, "We know you've tried very hard, son, and that you've made the right decision now. We're with you all the way."

Some parents really rise to the occasion with a compassion and understanding they may never have revealed before.

# Your Brothers, Sisters, and Other Relatives

We've found that brothers and sisters are usually tremendously understanding and supportive. This has been consistently true not only for separated clients and friends we've known, but it has also been true for each of us as well. Both Dick's brothers and sisters-in-law were very accepting of his new status and were prepared to welcome him along with a new partner when he visited each of them recently. And David's brother has been supportive from the beginning, helping to make things easier for David by acting as an intermediary with other, less sympathetic relatives.

Not everyone may be as fortunate as we've been, but in most instances, your siblings will probably come through for you. Part of the reason brothers and sisters seem to be able to be so helpful is that they seldom have a great investment in your marriage being a tremendous "success." They're probably used to your getting into trouble from time to time, so they can jump in and give you a shot of loving when you need it without any conditions attached. But whatever the reasons, they're a joy for whom we can be grateful.

Other relatives are often another story. Their loyalties may be closer to other people than yourself—to *their* brothers and sisters, your parents, for example. And they may take their cues from them. If your parents are giving you a hard time, they're likely to follow suit. Ian's troubles with his parents, which you may recall from our earlier discussion, were compounded in just this way.

Ian had always been extremely close to his father's brother, and his uncle had frequently invited Ian to stay at his house. It was almost as if the uncle and aunt were another set of parents. Indeed, they acted like Ian's own parents at the time of his separation, refusing to have anything further to do with him even though they might have helped Ian a great deal. Ian's letters to them went unanswered just as they had to his own parents. And his pleas for help in mending his tattered relationship with his parents were also ignored.

Like Ian's previous sad story, however, this one also had a happy ending, because along with reconciliation with his parents went improvement in his relationship with his uncle and aunt. Since your parents' behavior may serve as a good barometer of how your other relatives are going to react to your separation, it may be wise to anticipate their responses on the basis of your observations of your parents. Don't count on them to ignore their own social network in responding to your predicament. With luck, your folks will treat you better than Ian's and so will your other relatives.

# Your In-laws

## Former In-laws

The range of responses of in-laws to the separation and divorce of their daughter and son-in-law is tremendously varied. But this is one set of relationships where you really can take the initiative. If, for example, you've never liked your in-laws and hated seeing them at family gatherings, you'll never have to see them again. And come to think of it, that's only fair because they probably won't want to see you either.

This is not to say that you should be nasty to them or say unkind things about them to your children; they are your kids' grandparents after all and you may want to protect that relationship for their sake. But you are under no obligation to endure heavy trips your former in-laws may feel like laying on you. And you should be able to expect some consideration in return for your respect.

One poor boob we know drove his kids miles to see their maternal grandmother, figuring he'd read a book and have a cup of coffee at her house while she spent the time with her grandchildren. As soon as he got the kids to the door, his ex-mother-in-law asked when he'd be back to pick up his children. He felt as if she saw him as merely a shuttle service for her grandchildren. Of course, after a day spent in the local drugstore staring out at the rain, our fearless father vowed never to make that trip again.

On the other hand, you and your in-laws may have had a good relationship while you were married to their daughter. If that's true, and if both you and they can get over the initial discomfort caused by the separation (perhaps by talking about it), there's no reason why you can't continue the relationship.

## New In-laws

New or prospective in-laws are a special problem for the separated father because they tend to view a divorced man with children as a high-risk person for their daughter to marry. They're often unsure of how they should act with this strange species and may be awkward and uncomfortable with you. If you give them time, though, they'll probably come around. They'll get used to seeing you with their daughter and they won't think of you as anything worse than the usual pig in a poke.

But seriously, we know a number of cases where new in-laws have been extremely loving and understanding and have in effect become another set of grandparents for the separated father's children. It's really nice having these people pulling for you, and your kids probably won't mind a new source of birthday presents either.

# Your Friends

We've said quite a bit already about your friends' reactions to your separation. They run the gamut from support to outright rejection. But in all cases, in one way or another, there will be some kind of change in each of these relationships. There has to be, because *you* are changing, and not just your marital or social status. You are undergoing a stressful situation which is bound to affect you, and you may also be experiencing simultaneously even more profound, developmental changes, stimulated or represented by your separation. Of course, your friends will react to these changes.

From your perception, however, it may be your friends who seem to be doing all the changing—all you are doing is suffering.

But because you *are* suffering and vulnerable and bereft of some of your loved ones, you'll become more dependent on certain of your friends for comfort, support, and love. Because you're confused by what has happened you may also turn to them for advice and understanding. You may want to be exonerated, forgiven, and confirmed by them. And yet, you'll want *them* to remain the same!—even though you've changed and your social contracts with them have changed. Few friends are capable of the impeccable behavior required by these conflicting demands.

For friendships that bordered on acquaintanceship, geared more to your social roles as husband, father, golf partner, or dinner host, your various changes may spell the end. The reasons given or inferred by you for this may be painful at first, but you'll soon learn to accept these losses and begin finding new friends to replace them.

Really close, emotional friendships are much more difficult. You'll be keenly sensitive to every nuance of response to you because really close friends are precious—you may feel that they mustn't be lost. You will be more vulnerable to their opinions of you, and more anxious about what they think of your behavior. If "correct" responses aren't forthcoming almost immediately from these friends, you're likely to be deeply hurt and angry. What is especially difficult for the friendship is that often you'll be too involved in your own pain and confusion to be able to see things from your friends' point of view and to appreciate their reasons for reacting the way they do. You probably won't be very forgiving.

And your friends are likely to give you something to feel hurt and unforgiving about, because few of them will be innocent. It's hard for most people to avoid being judgmental in these situations, even if, or especially if, they love you. Your friends may also count on you in lots of ways and resent you for being too tied up emotionally by your separation to be available to them the way you used to. So they may be angry with you as well as sympathetic. It's a lot to expect them to be *only* supportive and loving when their reactions are likely to be quite complex. Friends may also find an "either for or against me" sort of stance a heavy trip for a friend to lay on *them*.

Divided loyalties, bearing some similarity to the excruciating division of the children by the parting couple, create an especially difficult path for friends to tread. It is extremely difficult for anyone to divide attentions to the couple equitably enough to suit either member, and besides, anything diminished may be unforgivable. Guards against being disloyal to one may so restrict responsiveness to the other as to make social ease impossible—intolerable for a friendship that has been warm and open. Conversation may have to steer clear of anything remotely relevant to anyone—particularly the separation, the former spouse, or a new companion, changing previous intimacy into distance and painful trivialities. It is an intolerable situation for everyone. Unless there is a clear decision about "custody" of the friends in question, and visiting rights perhaps, this situation may prove too awkward and unrewarding for anyone to maintain. It will be much easier to find a fresh start with someone else.

Yet some friendships weather all of these storms, not without a battering perhaps, but with a will. This is because some friendships grow along with the people involved. Many of the phenomena we've mentioned—the pain and "betrayal" and loss—are a consequence of the changes in ourselves, and our friends, and in our circumstances. It's well to respect these experiences, but they needn't be impassable barriers to a friendship—a new one.

A new person (which is what you'll be as you go through these changes) requires new friendships. And some of these may be found among the old ones if the process of mourning the loss of the old relationship can be accomplished while retaining a vision of the new one. If both people grow and are ready to accept even their worst reactions to each other as merely part of the process of change, their friendship can survive anew. It may even improve.

# Your New Companion

Although we may have created an impression of the separated father as being entirely alone in the world, we're happy that it usually isn't so. Most men eventually find someone to share their lives with, if they haven't already done so before they separate. We know most of us are a lot happier and healthier within the warmth and protection of a stable and loving relationship; this kind of relationship may be especially welcome to divorced men with children.

But many separated fathers experience a lot of complications and difficulties when they begin to establish a close relationship with "another woman"—some of them imaginary and some very real. Some problems arise for your new relationship because of the various emotional reactions you're likely to go through as a result of separation. Other difficulties more specifically relate to your new companion's reactions to your kids (and to you as a "father"), as well as your children's responses to her. And finally, as a consequence, there are the complications and problems associated with being caught in the middle between your children and your new companion.

## Your New Companion and Your Separation

During the first year of your separation, a new companion will probably be surprised to find herself having to comfort you more than she ever imagined, encountering more grief than she might have expected you to experience. If so, the surprise will probably come for both of you because neither of you will have counted on your feelings being so strong. This often happens because of the tendency to focus primarily on the separation from your wife at first, overlooking, as a consequence, the powerful but often delayed impact of your separation from a family—a whole complex of severed bonds.

Your woman friend may be unprepared for the painful mourning process that follows, particularly trying for her because it emphasizes the strength and importance of the bonds that have been broken. In some cases she may have to witness not only the normal catastrophizing and grief, but be expected to put up with desertions as well, since reconciliation fantasies are quite common at this stage in the mourning process. Some men may actually "run back" to their ex-wives temporarily. Even though this behavior may be normal under the circumstances, it certainly demands a lot from a new relationship. And it's embarrassing and awkward for the separated father trying to explain his behavior to his lover, particularly when he usually doesn't know what's going on himself.

Her concerns about her security in a relationship with you are understandable under the circumstances, but unfortunately, these concerns may also prompt her to welcome antagonistic relations between you and your former wife. Uniting in hostility toward your ex-wife may serve to cement your new relationship, but it can also work against co-operative interactions with the children's mother and interfere with your need to function effectively as a father. So it's in your own interests both as a partner and as a father to be as respecting and caring as you can when your new companion reacts with anxiety about the stability of your relationship.

## Your New Companion and Your Kids

Once most of the hassle and grieving of separation are done, and you've recovered your "lost" children, still further adventures await you and your new companion. The following scenarios may not fit your particular case, especially if your friend comes equipped with kids herself, but it's the most common and the one we know best.

To begin with, though your new companion may have known you had kids (and there are a few instances in which even that was kept as a surprise), it probably never sank in that you might be a *father*.

When you and your woman friend first met, your kids probably weren't in the picture, and you were only a couple—just the two of you. Then suddenly along come your kids. And just as suddenly your hitherto supportive and comforting companion may become "unaccountably" surly or even downright hostile toward your relationship with the kids.

Unwelcome and perplexing as her reactions may be to you, they will probably be natural and understandable responses to the disappointment, for instance, of losing the privacy you had enjoyed together as a couple. While you may gain love and affection from your children as compensation, she may only become heir to a difficult and unrewarding situation, and not all of it due to the kids! When the kids arrive on the scene, she may suddenly find herself a social embarrassment and a problem to *you*. Recently separated fathers are often self-conscious about having a new companion. They become totally preoccupied with fantasies about what their kids will think and say about their dad's having a "girl friend," and may turn all their attention to coping with these often imaginary problems.

Both of your intrepid authors, for instance, worried unnecessarily about how their children would describe their fathers' friends to their schoolmates. Not surprising to us now, our kids handled this "problem" with ease, referring quite matter-of-factly to "Daddy's friend" or "my dad's girl friend," a simple and straightforward description of the relationship.

Our behaviour under these circumstances is usually funny in retrospect, but, dead serious at the time, it may be very unfunny to our "girl friends." Imagine her feelings, for example, if her partner always takes his kids out on visiting days and says he doesn't want to bring the children home to meet her "until the time is right."

Another case in point is the father who actually persuaded his companion to stay with a girl friend—to clear out of her own apartment!—when his kids came for the weekend. He thought it might be devastating to his children to discover that he was sleeping with someone other than their mother. But early one morning when the kids called, his companion answered the phone, and the game was up. When their dad got on the line they asked him if she had stayed the night—not as an accusation but out of simple curiosity. Their flabbergasted father sputtered and muttered, but had to admit finally that she had.

It's hard to imagine what he was thinking, or rather what he was thinking his kids were thinking. Surely they weren't interested in catching him at something or sitting in judgment on their father; they just wanted to know what was going on.

In most cases, even though the children's mother may be antagonistic toward the new woman in your life, the kids are often quite willing to establish a relationship with her. They may even become loyal friends. To illustrate the point: one mother scolded her kids because they wanted to call up their father's friend when he was out of town. They insisted on calling her anyway, asserting that she was their friend, too, and that they had every right to speak to her if they wanted. This kind of response can be very heartening to someone in the vulnerable and usually unofficial position of the "girl friend."

A new mate or companion is in an unenviable position, even if she has the official status of a new wife. She's usually the odd-woman-out when the kids are around, especially if time with the children is at a premium. So the game of musical chairs is often rigged against her by a real or imagined coalition between father and kids. She can pretend she doesn't feel excluded, moving even farther away from reality and from you, or she may accept the situation and make whatever adjustments she can. In either case it's no bargain.

When the kids appear on the scene she's faced with role conflicts as well. She can adopt the role of mother, if it's available, and attempt to form a new family unit, or she can try to maintain a separate (adult) relationship with the father which does not include being "mom." Either is tough to do, because on the one hand she'll have a hard time winning full acceptance as a new parent, and on the other, she'll find that equanimity and a stance of uninvolvement are all but impossible in the midst of a single-parent madhouse.

For the separated father, having another adult around can be a great help, whatever her status, contributing a much-needed and probably more objective point of view in the middle of all the confusion, not to mention a handy baby-sitter on occasion.

At times the separated father's woman friend can provide needed firmness and structure when a vacuum is created because dad is busy playing the role of a harried and ignored mother to his children.

But this kind of contribution isn't always appreciated. The separated father is often loath to accept anyone else disciplining his kids, not only because he tends to guard his parental prerogatives jealously, but also because he may feel terribly disloyal to his children if he abandons them to further mischief at the hands of a "stranger." Ouch. Obviously this won't do.

The separated father must learn to share responsibility with his new mate and be ready to welcome her involvement when she offers it even if it means having to face his own irrational feelings about his children. Trusting your partner and her judgment with the children is important for your new relationship and necessary if you want to create the kind of healthy and balanced household your kids can thrive in.

But the children's father isn't the only one who will try to regulate his new companion's involvement with the children. His ex-wife will often be personally antagonistic to this interloper, and dead set against her intruding on the mother's territory vis-à-vis the children. The father is usually caught in the middle, having to mediate between his ex-wife and his new partner. What's more, he usually shares some of his ex-wife's feelings of territoriality at first, yet he also has to make a case for his companion's need and right to function as a responsible adult with the children.

His new mate's position is clearly a very vulnerable one. While the father is in an even more difficult position, being in the middle, he is, by the same token, in a more powerful one than his new partner because everyone pivots around him. It is essential, therefore, that the separated father does understand his new mate's situation as well as his own; he controls her relations with others in this system to a great extent. He needs to be able to empathize with her—to see the world through her eyes rather than being defensive. It may be hard at first, but some perspective is necessary or he'll spend all his time bouncing back and forth between one untenable position and another, feeling disloyal and unfair to one person or another.

The trick is actually to listen, without becoming guilty and feeling defensive as hell, when she tells you how it is. You don't have to agree or side with her about everything; you owe respect to your own views too and she doesn't have your responsibilities and problems to contend with as a parent. It's also true that she may not be as empathic as you'd like her to be, particularly if your defensiveness prevents her from knowing how things really are for you. But she's your friend—hear her out.

## Caught in the Middle

If the separated father begins to sound like a schmuck vis-à-vis his new mate, it usually isn't because he sets out to be that way. He probably has it in mind for everyone to like each other and to be nice, and for everyone to live happily ever after; he's had enough misery. But the cast usually refuses to follow his script; they pull him instead in conflicting directions according to their own needs. He feels caught in the middle, unable to satisfy all of their competing demands, and wonders why he feels so bad when he's surrounded by the people he loves.

The trouble is that he usually tries to do too much. Feeling pulled and pushed by everyone else's needs, he actually tries to orchestrate everyone's lives and the relationships between his children and his new mate. Because he's sensitive to their feelings, or his perception of their feelings, and wants them all to be happy, he gets hooked into feeling responsible for everybody, for whether or not they like each other, or have a good time, or are co-operative. And he's bound to do a lousy job of it, making himself miserable in the process.

The point of the matter is that it can't be done. You can't direct all the traffic. You may have to take the rap for your choice of partner and for choosing to have children, but you can't assume responsibility for the way they choose to react to these things. You may be fortunate enough to have a new mate who isn't defensive, who likes kids, and who can interact with them easily. Unthreatened by your attention to your children, she may readily establish her own, independent relationship with them. On the other hand, you may not be quite so lucky. Your new partner may have no idea of how to interact with children; she may not even like them and may see them only as competition for your time.

However it appears to you, you're going to have to give your new partner and your children the time and space to sort things out for themselves. That's their business and their responsibility. Maybe things won't be great to begin with, but they'll probably go a lot smoother if you concentrate on enjoying yourself with each of them and worrying less about what they're doing with each other.

We know one separated father who worried constantly about his kids and his friend having a good time together. He figured that if they really enjoyed themselves, they'd be bound to like each other and that it was up to him to bring this about. He nearly ended up with an ulcer and made himself thoroughly unhappy before he realized what he was doing.

Here's an example: Henry would plan some activity for himself and his kids and hope that Marianne would come along with them. But she seldom did, and he noticed he wasn't having a good time playing with the kids, because he'd be worried that Marianne was sitting at home angry because she'd been left out. Often he was right;

she was. Finally, when he screwed up his courage and asked her about it, she said she didn't like to butt in on his time with the kids and felt like an intruder if she wasn't specifically invited to join them.

So Henry tried a new tactic. Every time he planned an outing he issued a special invitation to Marianne. Because she had been invited, Marianne felt obliged to go, and ended up becoming angry on the scene instead of at home. She still felt left out. She had never been asked what she'd like to do, and she often found she didn't like doing the outdoorsy kinds of things Henry and the kids had planned.

After one of these unsuccessful expeditions during which Marianne had spent most of the day complaining, Henry threw up his hands. He told Marianne that she was welcome to come with them but in the future she'd have to pick and choose her own spots. If she didn't like what they were going to do, it was perfectly all right, and she didn't have to come if she didn't want to.

At the same time, Henry admitted to himself that there were things he liked to do with Marianne that were no fun for the kids, like going for a walk or dropping in on friends (as well as a few other things requiring more privacy). He decided that if he felt like doing these things with Marianne, he *would,* even if the kids happened to be around.

Both decisions were made defiantly and undiplomatically, but they began to get Henry off the hook. And when some of the pressure was off, Henry found it much easier to be less defensive and more genuinely interested in finding out in what ways his companion actually wanted to be involved.

There are two traps into which the separated father can fall in the kind of situation Henry faced. The first danger is that of becoming too caught up in trying to be a wonderful father to notice the impact on your companion. It may never have occurred to Henry, for instance, that by consistently planning activities that he knew his new mate disliked, he thereby effectively excluded her from participating. If he had honestly wanted her to join them he probably would have included her in planning the events in the first place.

The second pitfall is being *overly* concerned with the feelings of your new mate—to the point of ignoring the needs and wishes of your children. This second trap is often particularly insidious and potent because the father, having "failed" in one relationship, may work extra hard to appease his new companion in order to make a go of the new relationship.

Finding a balance between two opposing pulls on him—from his kids on one hand and his new companion on the other—may be extremely difficult. Moreover, because he's been burned, the separated father may not actually try wholeheartedly to bring everyone together at first anyway, even if children and partner want it.

Instead, he may actually try to keep each of them separate. Because he is still recovering from the trauma of separation from his children, he may be afraid to risk what remains of his relationship with them by sharing his kids fully with his new companion, especially if he's uncertain about how well his new companion will be able to relate to them.

For similar reasons he may want to protect his new relationship from his kids. Wanting and needing someone for himself, he may be afraid that his new companion won't like them and may worry about whether or not his new relationship will be able to handle the strain of children. As a consequence, the separated father may adopt the policy of divide and conquer—or survive at least, until things mellow out.

Of course, the situation is actually more complicated than we've presented it thus far, because there are more people involved and more things at stake. The separated father will tend to guard his time with his children for reasons other than protecting one relationship from the other. For one thing, he already has to share the kids with his ex-wife, probably getting a small slice of their time at that. For another, he may want to protect the children from the pain of a second separation if the new relationship doesn't work out. He may also prize his new status as a parent, and value his new housekeeping skills, and be unwilling to share them with another person, even if he may have learned some of them from that person. As a result, the newly separated father may feel anything but generous.

But that's not all. By virtue of the fact that he is in the middle, the separated father is in a position to control and moderate his new mate's relationships with the children, and not always just so he can have the kids all to himself. It's all too easy for him to use his relationship with the children as a weapon against his companion, making the kids his allies and confidants, running off with them when the going gets hot with her, and so on. He can also subvert whatever authority he may have delegated to her with the children, winking at the kids, for example, when she tries to upbraid them for something.

Thus, while it is foolhardy for separated fathers to think they are responsible for everyone else's feelings just because they're in the middle, it's equally shortsighted if they fail to appreciate what a potentially unfair advantage this pivotal position affords them in their relationship with a new companion. They need to be scrupulous in how they handle both of these aspects if they wish to have harmonious relations with both kids and partner.

Beginning anew with someone is often a bumpy road for the separated or divorced man with children. There are so many pitfalls, so many pressures and anxieties. It's easy to get bogged down and to make mistakes and so difficult to find a path that's satisfactory to everyone. Yet people manage to do it.

So relax. Don't try to orchestrate everyone. Acknowledge your responsibility as a central figure, but expect them to have some recognition of their responsibility for themselves and for how things go for all of you.

Make sure you consult your partner in making arrangements regarding the children that will also affect her, like adding on additional visiting time or having the kids on an "off" weekend when the two of you may have had other plans. After all, she has a right to a say in your life together.

Cherish your relationship and give it some special care. Set aside some time for the two of you to do things without the kids—regularly, so you can count on it. And make sure you create some space just for yourself, so you don't build up a personal energy debt by responding to everyone else's needs. With some time and care things can work out okay.

## The Daddy Sandwich

Dick likes to recall the way in which his son Robbie used to come running whenever he and his new partner, Bonnie, started to hug each other. Rob would come up behind Dick, encircling him with his arms, competing openly with Bonnie for his father's affection. But it wasn't only competitive. You could see there was something Robbie liked about the open display of affection that had prompted him to join in in his one-sided way to make what he called the "Daddy sandwich."

After a while—still from behind his father—Robbie's arms began to include Bonnie in their hug, making a love sandwich of Daddy, which even little Samantha soon couldn't resist.

It's clear that if kids are to learn about love and affection and hugging and kissing, they need to see it happen to people they love. They don't have that opportunity any more between their natural parents, but they still need to learn that loving relationships are possible between men and women. So don't be too shy about finding and loving someone other than their mother, and to allow your children to share in that love.

# *Your Job and Fellow Workers*

Both separation and fathering require time and energy, much of which will have to come from other areas of your life, most notably your work and recreation. The sobering effects of separation make it easy to give some things up, like bowling or golf or model-building. These activities may lose their interest temporarily as you become caught up in more basic personal dramas. But your work is probably more sacred. In addition to keeping you afloat financially, it may be a place of refuge from the more confusing emotional problems of separation, and a source of much-needed self-esteem. Knowing that you can still function on your job, in spite of the feeling that the rest of your life is going down the tube, can literally be a lifesaver.

But if you cling to this life raft after the crisis is over, you'll have a hell of a time fathering your children. Furthermore, if you don't begin to spend time with your kids, it's possible that you'll generate so much guilt and remorse about being a "bad" father that you may have to jump off the raft and drown yourself in your work, keeping too busy to feel anything. Ouch.

Obviously, we don't want to encourage that kind of self-defeating cycle. On the contrary, we think one of the potential benefits of separation is a restructuring of your priorities, in which fathering and family begin to compete more favorably with work. We aren't just thinking of duty and the avoidance of guilt. Shifting some of your priorities in favor of the kids can be immensely rewarding. Here is one of our latest examples.

Dick's five-year-old daughter knows "he's making a book" and that he teaches people, so she has some idea of what he does for a living. But her first answer to a dentist's unsuspecting question was a gratifying example of how she perceives his priorities. "What does your father do, Samantha?" Sam's reply: "He cuddles me."

Nevertheless, it's a good idea if your kids know what you do for a living so they can learn something about the world of work, and so that they'll know more about you and your life. Take them to work with you and show them around. Let them see what you do, and how you do it, if that's possible. Introduce them to the people you spend so much of your time with—people who may only be names to your children otherwise. There are many advantages to bringing your working life and your life with the children together so each has some appreciation of the other.

At the same time your kids learn about you and your colleagues at work, your children will also become known to your employers and your fellow workers. It's an excellent way to make your commitment to the kids known to these people. Familiarity with your kids will help them to understand and support your efforts as a father, even if it means some changes in you at work. It will make it easier for you to pass up lunches with them, for instance, so you can get your work done early enough to pick up the kids at school. They may be willing to accept your working overtime in order to take a day off to be with your kids to see them perform in a school play or on the baseball diamond, or to meet with your children's teachers for a conference.

These days many men, whether divorced or not, are beginning to temper their vocational ambitions with their family's need for stability and their own need to spend more time with their children. If you turn down job changes that could eat up your time with the kids, or refuse promotions that require moving away from them, there will be some basis for understanding and respect for your decisions, particularly if you have already established yourself as a father with your employers and colleagues.

There's much you can do to find time from your work to be with your children, even if it seems like an impossible task at first. Once you've made a commitment to fathering, discovering and inventing ways to do it will become second nature to you.

While we ourselves are fortunate in that our jobs provide a great deal of flexibility, we know from the experiences of others that adjustments in work schedules can be made in even the most rigid of jobs. As we've already mentioned, people skip lunches to make sure they get away in time to pick up their kids. Or they may spend their lunch hours with their children instead of at work. Other separated fathers opt to work overtime to compensate for time spent with their children during regular working hours, or in some cases arrange to do some of their work at home.

Those who can't rearrange their jobs find other ways to cover the

gaps that exist between the
Some find baby-sitters to g
children until their fathers
shift have more trouble, l
enough visiting schedules t
thers take advantage of be
with their children.

In some rare cases fathe
of sync with their kids, ac
patible line of work. But
for the time by ensuring tl
their kids. Many become
cooking and keeping hou
occasions to be with the
they're spending more time with their children now than they ever
had before.

# Children's Teachers and
## School

School is one of the most important and dominant factors in children's lives, broadening and shaping their experiences for many years. Schools become heir to our children, not only teaching new skills, but also taking over many of the functions of parents: inculcating ideals and values, mediating relationships with the world and other people, and simply looking after our children every school day for most of the year.

We rely heavily on the schools to take over many of the burdens of child rearing, and we in turn transfer much of our authority as parents to the schools, supporting their functioning as our surrogates and the teachers' work as educators.

In a sense we lose our children to the school system, and we're usually glad of it, especially if we've had the kids underfoot a great deal. Our children's careers as students free us to do lots of other things. In the special instance of divorced parents it permits mothers to return to the adult world of work so they can support themselves and it allows separated fathers, already in the work force, to accept the responsibilities of parenting their children realistically.

But obviously, whatever their convenience to us, schools have the enormously more important task of teaching our children the skills and attitudes they will need to survive and succeed in society. Yet as important as school is to our children's welfare and to our own, often we abandon our roles as guides and protectors once they begin school even though they still need us to help them cope as people with the often impersonal machinery of education. No school or teacher can be expected to give your children the individual attention they may need at various times.

Fathers too often see school-related activities as lying within their wife's area of responsibility. Beyond reading written summaries (report cards) and infrequently attending an occasional conference with the teacher to discuss their child's progress, most fathers are out of it;

they have no idea what's going on with their kids at school. The schools are used to this and so are most mothers and children. Eventually, no one really expects dads to be involved at all.

It's a pity because there are many things fathers can do to help make school a good experience for their children, both in terms of their learning and their relationships with other people. Whether you know physics and chemistry is less important than your interest in your kids' learning.

Most of us can remember traumatic confrontations with other kids or with terrifying and tyrannical teachers (or so they appeared to us) when we would have appreciated the support and backing of our fathers. All too many of these events that shaped our lives and affected the way we see and think about ourselves took place outside the guidance and protection of our parents. What wouldn't we have given to have had someone around to help us?

Perhaps one of the reasons so many fathers avoid involvement with the schools, and particularly elementary schools, is because they view education as a woman's province, just as it was in their day. It's a fact that a child's earliest experiences at school are still almost exclusively with women teachers, and fathers, themselves products of this system, may be too embarrassed to step into this "woman's world." Yet by their avoidance, they also deny to their children the missing and needed male influence that they could provide.

Unfortunately, no one seems to take a father's role in education seriously; fathers in our culture just aren't expected to be involved with the schools. But if the situation is generally wanting, imagine what it's like for the separated father and his children.

## Separated Fathers Are Out

In the absence of information to the contrary, the school will assume that as a separated father you are *out,* and they probably won't ask you if that's the case or not. If the parents of one of their pupils are separated or divorced the school authorities, like everyone else in our society, will take it for granted that the mother has custody and that the father is out of the picture. Here is one example which illustrates the power of some of these assumptions:

By chance a father discovered that his son had been given a battery of aptitude and intelligence tests at the mother's request. The father had not been consulted about the testing nor had he been given any feedback on the results. He was about to be similarly excluded from important decisions about his son's education based on the results of the testing when he finally learned about it.

Despite the fact that he and his involvement with his children were well known to the school authorities, he was told by them that they had assumed that he had "no legal right" to feedback or any say in the decisions that they might make about his son. They hadn't bothered to check out their assumptions, however, and discovered to their embarrassment that in this instance they had been entirely wrong. The father in question shared legal custody of the children and had every right to be involved.

To be fair, however, the schools draw their assumptions on the basis of experience as well as prejudice. In most instances, the mother has in fact been awarded custody and is legally the parent to whom the school is responsible. As one school principal put it, "It's really sad for the fathers. Lots of them have problems with their ex-wives and aren't allowed to see the kids. But we can't do very much to help them."

This same principal, although sympathetic to the feelings of separated fathers and their children, also pointed out that very few fathers actually seemed to be involved enough with their kids to attempt to establish a relationship with the school, whether it was legally possible for them to do so or not. Hence, for one reason or another, good or bad, school authorities act on the assumption that separated fathers are out of the picture.

## Staying in the Picture

Unless there are actual legal restrictions against your doing so (in which case you may have to find a legal solution), there are many ways to stay in the picture. The following are some of the guidelines we have developed for ourselves through experience and through discussions with school authorities:

*Make yourself known* to the school. Go there and introduce yourself to the children's teachers, to the principal, and to anyone else with whom your kids will be involved.

Let them know that you are separated or divorced and fill them in as best you can about what your situation actually is. If you have custody or joint custody, or any specified rights at all, make sure they know it because otherwise they'll assume you have none at all.

When you're introducing yourself, don't neglect to make yourself known to the secretarial staff, which handles the mailing of notices and deals with absences from school and so on. This is often a very important link in the communication chain.

*Ask to be specifically included on their regular mailing list* for information and announcements about school activities. Obtain a copy of their over-all timetable for the year if one is available so you can keep track of special activities. It's particularly helpful if you can anticipate in-service days when the school will be closed so that you can make plans that could include having the children. It's certainly no fun to discover at the last minute that special arrangements will have to be made because the kids aren't going to school.

Make sure you're informed about parent-teacher conferences, special testing or planning sessions for your children, as well as school plays, sports, and other events you might like to attend. And if you're overlooked even once, make an issue of it with the person responsible so he or she knows you're really serious about it.

Even so, you'll probably find that the school still tends to send most of the news to your former wife instead of to you. This is partly a simple consequence of the fact that most messages are sent home with the kids. If your kids stay at their mother's more often than your place, she'll naturally receive most of the hand-carried mail. The school may be nice enough to mail notices to you, but frequently the messages arrive too late.

Hence, you need to maintain good communications with your former wife. Ask her to check with you to make sure you've received notices of special importance: conferences with teachers, in-service days when school will be closed, a need for special clothing or equipment, bag lunches for class picnics, and so on. And if you should happen to get the information first, be sure to notify her. Your kids will appreciate it and so will the school.

*Be as supportive as you can* of the school's efforts to educate your children. Remember, as a parent you potentially have a great deal of impact on your children's teachers, some of whom may feel vulnerable to your evaluations and criticism. Don't be afraid to tell them what you think will be helpful to their work with your child, but try to remain on the teacher's side as well. Teachers have a difficult job, and they're more likely to do it well (to your child's benefit) if they feel your appreciation and support.

*Be a responsible parent.* Get the kids to school on time if you're dropping them off. It may take some special effort on your part to do so, but it will be worth it. You may have forgotten how very embarrassing it can be to a kid having to enter school after classes have begun. If you are late, see that your child has a note of explanation. Better still, if your child doesn't mind being seen with you (if he isn't an adolescent in other words), walk him up to class and apologize to the teacher for getting him to school late. Doing so can add a nice personal touch, underscoring your involvement with your kids.

Because there is often a lot of moving about from house to sitter's to school, the possibilities of some kinds of problems are multiplied for the children of separated parents. School books and homework may be left at the wrong house, putting your kids in the dog house with their teacher. And if they missed school while with one parent, they may need a note from the other parent or your kids will be left holding the bag without an excuse. Co-operation between parents in these matters will help, but the patience and forbearance of your children's teachers must also be enlisted so the kids don't suffer unfairly from their somewhat scattered circumstances.

*Participate.* Take part in the school events you asked to be informed about. Your kids will really appreciate seeing you in the audience when they're on stage or on the playing field. There may be some embarrassing or uncomfortable moments if their mother is attending the same event, but it makes no sense to avoid occasions that are important to your kids just because you're uptight around their mother. If it's really bad, you may want to make some kind of deal with her to take turns so you can both fully enjoy these times with your kids.

Make sure you have regular opportunities to talk to your children's teachers, whether they are formal parent-teacher conferences or not. It isn't necessary for you to wait to be invited to an officially scheduled meeting if you have something to discuss with a teacher. Teachers will probably welcome the opportunity to exchange information and ideas with you about your kids.

It's especially important that you have input into the school's evaluation and decision-making processes concerning your children. You provide a different point of view based on your intimate knowledge of them. So you can help the teacher to see your child through your eyes, opening up new possibilities for the teacher with your child.

There are other fun ways of getting inside the school and being more a part of your children's lives besides the usual modes by which most parents relate to school. Dick attended kindergarten, for instance, in order to see what school was like for Robbie. He spent half a day a week serving as a helper to the teacher and he loved every minute of it. Although his attendance diminished somewhat in later grades he still feels at home in his children's school, comfortable enough to drop in every now and then for an afternoon in class or a chat with the teachers. And his recent slide presentation of a colorful South American trip was a hit with both his son's third grade class and with his daughter's kindergarten class.

So, there are lots of ways you can find to participate in your children's education. Just because you're separated doesn't mean you have to be excluded. You'll probably discover that keeping tabs on what's going on for your kids at school will make you feel even better about your relationship with them. It will allow you to have greater input into their lives and will give you a chance to contribute your own standards and values to their education.

# 3. Father as "Mother"—
## The Evolution of a Houseperson

### Getting Started

Few separated fathers realize that there might be more work to do after separation than before. Many may even have separated in the first place to escape from the boredom of being a husband and family man or in order to discover a more exciting life. Yet, judging from the separated couples we have seen, most husbands are ill-prepared for the responsibility of taking care of themselves, let alone their children. We've seen many a fantasy balloon of the free and easy bachelor life rudely burst by the reality of hungry, crying children.

The fact is, of course, that the separated father is not the swinging bachelor that he once might have been or might possibly be if he did not have and want his children. He is a single parent. As such he really finds himself with two jobs rather than the one he left—all the "traditional" duties of a mother as well as those of a father.

Once regular visits with the children begin, he finds that they have to be fed, and that he is the chief cook. And if his kids are sloppy eaters or play hard or stay overnight, he discovers that there are clothes to pick up, wash, and mend. Beds have to be made and bathing supervised. There is cleaning to be done, toys and playthings to be bought, and so on. All this in addition to the kinds of things that fathers are expected to do, like playing ball, going fishing, or just horsing around with the children.

It is not surprising that some separated fathers find the demands of taking care of their children overwhelming or even impossible at first. For these people, shorter and less frequent visits may be helpful, enabling them to maintain contact with their children without feeling inundated by their new responsibilities. But often separated fathers who are appalled in the beginning by their multiple responsibilities, learn to become effective housepersons and to enjoy caring for their children. What is more, these men find the process of learning to be an independent, responsible parent both exhilarating and liberating. Fathers with even the gravest doubts about their capabilities who plunge on because the alternative to being with their children is unbearable are often rewarded by the surprising discovery—surprising not only to themselves, but to their children, friends, and even their ex-wives—that they can manage quite well in their new roles.

In the sections which follow, we have tried to provide some help for the budding houseperson-father in getting started on the job. Although we have concentrated primarily on the practical aspects, we recognize the important part that attitudes and emotional reactions play in learning the job. Many men have to overcome deeply ingrained attitudes about doing so-called "woman's work" before they can begin learning the skills necessary for housekeeping and child care. Others feel deeply resentful about "having" to take care of themselves and their children. Frequently, these separated fathers have to fight through the inertia fostered by such sentiments in order to get on with the job of fathering.

Even if he isn't hung up in these ways, the fledgling houseperson-father will probably have to cope with frequent surges of panic which arise because the situations he faces are novel and occur in an atmosphere that is usually emotionally charged with all kinds of feelings about separation, divorce, being a good parent, and so on. Catastrophizing under these circumstances is normal enough and understandable, even if it doesn't seem helpful. These reactions pass with time. Fortunately it doesn't seem to make much difference to the kids if their father squawks or gets himself excited about all the things he has to do. Emotional behavior is natural to them, and it won't be the first time they've noticed their dad is a sorehead, a jerk, or whatever your kids happen to call you.

Certain of the things we suggest may reduce your difficulties somewhat by preparing you to cope with at least some of the practical aspects of setting up a household. Mainly, we hope that our suggestions will encourage you to find your own creative solutions to the various problems you encounter. We do expect you to get excited from time to time if something looks impossible to you and at such times we hope you'll find something helpful in these pages. If not, you may find it helpful to throw this book on the floor or against a wall with sufficient force to give you relief. Additional copies may be purchased for this purpose.

## Room for Your Kids

Children need space and privacy for themselves. You need privacy too, especially if you have a roommate. So, if you can afford it, even if it means really stretching your budget, have a room in your home that the kids can call their own—one they can decorate and play in, clutter up and retire to. A private room will give them a haven from you when they need it and a place where you can send the kids when you're fed up with them. A separate room is useful for small children's naps and tantrums, and particularly to contain the messes that kids can make. If you can't stand the wreckage that they create, you can shut the door on it, helping them to clean it up when you feel up to the task.

We think the best reason for having a room for your kids, though, is the good feeling that it brings both you and your children—knowing that you belong together, that your home is their home and not just a place they visit.

## Furnishing the Children's Room

The kind of furniture you chose for your children's room is dependent in part on what you can afford and on what you and your kids like. We prefer regular beds, for example, probably because they are more homey to us. Other fathers and their kids decide on sleeping arrangements ranging from fold-out sofas, especially if the apartment is very small, to cots. Some kids find sleeping bags and air mattresses full of adventure. Younger children often love to sleep with their papa and occasionally it might be fun, but they should definitely have some sort of bed of their own. Aside from encouraging independence, separate beds will enable you to get some sleep, especially if your kids are squiggling, sideways sleepers as Dick's children are.

Storage space for kids' toys, tools, and materials is very helpful and makes housekeeping easier. Even two-year-olds can put their toys back in a box and they often get a kick out of giving their dad a hand. Toy boxes are particularly useful for this purpose. You can buy them or if you want to you can make your own. You'll find plans in those do-it-yourself furniture books. If you don't feel quite that ambitious, an old, brightly painted trunk will serve admirably as a toy chest. If you need chests of drawers or other items, unfinished furniture can be painted to match the toy box, and as time goes on you might want to add some extras like a desk and a chair or two. You may not have to do all of this yourself either. Kids love to help build and paint things, so we try to let our kids do as much as they can.

Chances are that you won't have as much money to spend as you did before your separation, so wise bargain hunting, painting, or refinishing furniture might turn out to be a necessary adventure. Many fathers we know get a kick out of their new-found skills as bargain hunter, painter, or carpenter, and being active in this way seems to counter the all too prevalent feelings of helplessness that often occur in the early stages of separation. It is hard to feel worthless, rotten, or guilty as you get the kids' room together.

But don't expect oohs and aahs from your kids. If things are going right, you're likely to find that they take it for granted. After all, fathers can do most anything.

"Hey doesn't that new desk look great! What do you think, son?"

"Yeah, it looks terrific, Dad." So what if he's a little amused by your enthusiasm?

By the way, even if your creations don't come out as you envisioned them, sleek and professional-looking, and they seldom do, it doesn't mean that your kids won't like them. Kids are usually sensitive to the feeling behind something made especially for them.

Now, if you really don't know a paint brush from a hammer or haven't a place to use them, making furniture or fixing it might not be for you. If cost is a consideration, looking through the classified ads in your local paper should turn up some really good secondhand furniture. Chasing down ads or finding great buys in new furniture is actually an exhilarating experience for some people as well as a practical necessity. If you can arrange it, take your kids on the hunting expedition; they'll really enjoy helping to pick things out for their room.

## Playthings

Even before you've furnished a room for your children, you'll probably want some things for your kids to play with when they come over—things that will be there when they come and will remain when they leave, things that will keep them busy while you attend to household chores, and things that you and your kids will have fun playing with together.

It is probably a good idea if many of the toys and materials remain a part of their place at your place. At first kids often wonder if they can take stuff "home" to their mother's and you might feel that you're being a bit childish and petty if you insist that certain items remain at your place. We suggest that you insist anyway. You'll save yourself a lot of trouble and resentment by adopting a policy right away as to what they can and can't take to their mother's.

For example, some things are just too big and cumbersome to haul around and others are too dear to you to see whisked away. And of course there are games you count on playing with your kids. So, if you want to make sure that those things are around when your kids come over, the best policy is to insist that they remain at your place. If you take the time to explain to your children why you'd like certain things to stay with you, they'll more than likely understand. If you respect your own feelings about this, after a while you'll probably find yourself feeling more generous about borderline cases. You may also find it helpful to have toys around that they can take with them when they leave, so you won't look completely selfish. If you need additional rationalization to assuage your guilt for appearing childish, just tell yourself that kids often get bored playing with the same toy all of the time, and that it's nice for them to be able to look forward to playing with something special at your place.

And incidentally, don't worry about that creepy feeling that might come over you that your kids don't really like you but just want to play with your toys. That's probably not true, you know.

But seriously, your kids are coming over to see you and to be with you, toys or no. If they happen to have a great time playing with some of the specialties of the house, that's an added bonus that you can enjoy too. In fact, you may soon wish that they'd play more with their toys rather than insisting on wrestling with you, although we must admit that those hugging, body-contact sports are probably the most satisfying of all.

As to games, we've found that our kids really enjoy ones that they can play with us, like cards or Monopoly or checkers or chess. But if you aren't a person who likes games, or if you don't know how to be a good sport when playing with your kids, especially when they cheat a bit, you can always get stuff that they can play by themselves.

Make sure that you get them things that you're willing to see them use. If you can't stand noise and clutter, for instance, don't try to override your feelings. A child can express herself just about as well on a toy guitar or accordion as she can on a set of drums or a horn. Bigger toys are easier to care for and less likely to get strewn around than are those with lots of tiny pieces. Huge pads of paper are great for drawing or painting and some judiciously placed newspaper can protect the rug or floor from normal spills and messes.

Incidentally, dressing the kids appropriately for play activities can save both work and money. An old shirt of yours will be an admirable smock for painting and it can double and triple as a bib when eating and an apron when your kids are old enough to help you cook.

When picking toys, try to keep tuned in to the things your kids really get excited about. Their criteria often will come as a surprise. Sure they're as likely to be conned by television advertising as you are and they may ask for things that only look good because of slow motion photography or tricky camera angles, or they may want something that will take a week of concentrated effort to put together. David once returned a bowling set with automatic pin placement an hour after he bought it. He and his kids were enthralled with the toy when they saw a demonstration of it on the tube. On opening it up, however, the instructions assured him that the lifetime of family fun would be well worth the seventy-two hours required to assemble it. But hard sell aside, kids do have a good idea of what they like to play with, and expensive or fancy toys are not always their idea of the best.

Dick remembers his great surprise one Christmas when a small deck of playing cards brought "wows" of delight and hugs of appreciation from his son, while bigger, more expensive presents were politely received. Playing cards with his dad was really important to Robbie and now his playing partner had given him a new deck of his own for them to play with. Getting what you really want at the right time is a thrill for any one of us. It will become clearer to you as it did to Dick that what your kids want isn't necessarily related to cost or size. It is a matter of what they are into at the moment. If it isn't cards, it may be things as simple as miniature tools, pens, pencils, or clothes. Staying turned in to your kids will help you be thoughtful and timely. You may find it helpful to keep a secret list of things that the kids have mentioned so you won't have to do any last-minute desperation shopping. It's a good idea for the other people in your life, too, come to think of it.

## Clothing

For the father who is used to having his wife outfit his children, clothing often presents a special problem. Because he is paying maintenance, he often continues to expect his ex-wife to buy all the clothing and to send along all necessary changes each visit. He may feel that his obligations are fulfilled when he sees to it that the kids change their clothes when they become dirty. He feels no compunction about stuffing these same dirty and wet clothes into an overnight bag and returning them to his ex-wife.

Needless to say, this arrangement can lead to a bit of resentment on the part of the former wife. She is still doing his laundry! We know of one case where the kids were going to stay with their father for two weeks. They arrived at his house with neatly packed suitcases of freshly washed clothes. In fact, the clothing was so freshly washed that it hadn't even been dried! In desperation, the father threw himself on the mercy of salespeople at a local department store and bought an entirely new wardrobe for both children.

Not every ex-wife who resents still being treated as chief servant will respond in such a dramatic fashion, but a lot of hassles and well-founded complaints of this sort can easily be avoided by a little planning on papa's part.

To begin with, go out and get a lot of underwear and socks for the children, and if you can afford it, an extra outfit or two as well. Children run through clean clothes quickly, getting them wet or dirty and even losing them. And it's no fun when you can't find something for them to wear when they need it.

To save yourself trouble, check the size labels on the clothes the kids have now and buy more of the same size. Of course, if your children are still small and tend to outgrow things quickly you may be wise to buy them clothes one size larger. You can usually return them if they don't fit. If you're still uncertain about sizes, ask the kids' mother. If you feel uncomfortable about doing that, salespeople in children's departments are generally very helpful to fathers, perhaps because male customers are still a novelty to them.

In addition to regular clothes, it is particularly satisfying to have the right kind of special purpose clothing on hand when the kids need it. Changes in the weather, wet clothing, or a spur of the moment decision to do something together make it really convenient to have tennis shoes, rubber boots, raincoats, or mittens around the house. And on a hot summer day, when you all feel like taking a swim, it's sure a lot nicer if you have bathing suits handy than it is to have to call up your ex-wife to see if you can pick up your kids' swimming suits.

A lot of things are accomplished by buying clothing for your kids besides keeping them from the cold. For one thing, you don't have to rely on the kids or their mother to remember to bring all of the right clothes, or to send enough of them. And if you have enough handy, you don't have to spend your time washing clothes in order to keep up with the dirty little rascals. If you have extra clothes, you can wash them later in the week when you do your own laundry. You can also spare yourself hassles by sending the kids back to their mother's with clean clothing you've bought, instead of returning dirty clothes stuffed in a bag.

Ultimately, building up your own wardrobe for the kids will save a lot of trouble hauling things back and forth, packing and unpacking. At the moment, it may look like a safari with all the things the kids need for a weekend. The process of picking the kids up or delivering them will also go more smoothly.

All of this will free both parents to send clothes with the kids' potential needs in mind rather than with hostility toward the other at heart. One caution. As clothes travel back and forth between households you may find yourself making invidious comparisons between "hers" and "yours," or grousing about the inevitable missing socks, faded or torn clothing, or "special" items that never seem to come back. Pride in your clothing selections for the kids is fine, and grouching to yourself is therapeutic, but a tug-of-war over the kids' clothes or possessions is no fun at all. After a while, you'll probably notice that the flow of clothing is pretty even, appreciate your ex-wife's restraint in not complaining when you lose socks or forget to send back mittens, and remember that the clothing really belongs to the kids. As time goes on, your kids will do pretty well, having a wardrobe in two places.

# Feeding Your Children

A client faced with separation recently expressed his concern about coping with his kids for the whole weekend. He couldn't see how he was going to feed them. Eating out all of the time didn't seem right. And he claimed that cooking was impossible for him. His therapist kidded him a bit about his catastrophizing, saying that he had nothing to worry about as long as he knew how to read. The therapist, a separated father himself, had recently recovered from his own bafflement about cooking. He knew that cooking only looked like a mystery to people who hadn't tried it. The therapist was confident that his client's block about feeding his children would probably vanish as soon as he discovered that he could follow recipes in a cookbook. So all he really needed was an ability to read recipes.

Far from reassured, the client protested that there had to be more to it than reading recipes because his wife seldom used cookbooks, yet still seemed magically to know what to do. And furthermore, she didn't even measure anything. Insistent on a magical explanation, the client couldn't see that his wife had simply remembered what to do after cooking the same things over the years, and he couldn't accept the idea that with practice he too would be able to cook with just as much nonchalance.

Cooking looked like an impossible task to this worried father, and further assurances probably wouldn't have allayed his anxiety; only experience could do that. Once he calmed down enough to follow a recipe himself, he would probably discover that he could cook. What is more, because the people who write the recipes are really good chefs, he would probably find himself an even better cook than he thought possible. At least that's what happened to his therapist, who even had nerve enough to publish some of his own recipes among those that follow later.

Before the neophyte chef can get around to overcoming his misgivings and practice cooking—assuming he isn't already a blue ribbon chef, incidentally—he still has the immediate problem of seeing to it that his hungry children eat something. Since responsibility for even thinking about food and its preparation is a new one for most ex-husbands, the thought of preparing dinner may come belatedly and as an unpleasant surprise. If you haven't planned ahead or done your shopping with the kids in mind, the thought of having to feed your children may even give rise to sudden panic. As long as you keep in mind that eating is what counts rather than fixing food and that your reputation as an adequate parent is not at stake merely because you've failed to prepare sumptuous and nutritious meals on time for your children, you'll be able to think of lots of alternatives to cooking. You can take them out for pizza, or chicken, or hamburgers and even if you think these quick-order places are plastic or squalid, for some reason the kids love them, and you'll be off the hook for a while.

When you're able to keep your head above water using these children-approved emergency measures, you can begin to relax a little, giving you enough time to plan ahead so that you and your children will be able to eat at home. After all, taking your kids out to eat every visit may be easy, but after a while we can almost guarantee that it will become incredibly boring. Besides, you would be missing out on the infinitely more relaxed atmosphere of home-cooked meals, especially if your kids are active, or if you are one of those fathers who gets embarrassed by the huge pile of compost which invariably builds up under the chairs of eating children.

There are intermediate steps that will allow you to prepare food at home without having to begin with five-course, candlelight dinners for your children. Aside from difficulty, cooking from scratch takes time, and you may want to spend more of your time with the kids than on food preparation at first, at least until you all feel comfortable with your new circumstances. So before you really get into the cooking scene, let's consider some simple ways of eating at home that don't require a lot of preparation.

## Easy Eating at Home

Leave food around for the kids to find! Bowls of fruit, shelled sunflower seeds, crackers, nuts, and so forth, can be put where your children can get to them easily. Milk and fruit juice can be kept on a low shelf in your refrigerator in cartons small enough for most kids to handle by themselves. In fact, if you like, you could set part of a refrigerator shelf aside just for the kids, where you can store hard-boiled eggs, cheese, and celery and carrots kept crisp in a glass or plastic container of ice water, and so forth. Kids over three years of age will eat what they can find when hungry (including junk food, remember), so with minimal planning and effort on your part you can make sure that they're getting things they need to eat. Incidentally, the found-food method will keep the kids out of your hair on Saturday and Sunday mornings, especially if they have games or toys to occupy them. They may even enjoy having the place to themselves, knowing they can always get hold of you.

For quick breakfasts, particularly on school days, you might try beating an egg in milk with cocoa or your favorite chocolate syrup and vanilla extract. Cereals are even easier. We try to avoid the sugar-coated ones, although sometimes our kids insist on them. You can slice a banana or other fruit on top, if your children will let you. Of course, there's always the old reliable toast, peanut butter and jelly, and a glass of milk.

If your kids have big morning appetites and get up early enough, you can give them the North American standard bacon (just fry over low heat and drain), and eggs. (Soft-boiled take only three or four minutes. David says you can prevent the eggs from breaking by making a small pin hole in the fat end before easing them into boiling water. Dick says baloney, the pin wouldn't go in.) Juice usually goes with this breakfast along with toast and milk, but if your kids don't like juices or they get tired of the same old thing, orange or apple slices may be a welcome alternative.

There are a host of easy possibilities for lunch. An abundance of foods are available which just need to be heated up, like ravioli, macaroni and cheese, beans, and soup. But the mainstay will probably be sandwiches. Salami, bologna, cheese, or peanut butter and jelly are all likely candidates. Or, if you feel like it, you can make hot dogs. Just boil them until they split, stick them in a bun, and let your kids put on the mustard, relish, sauerkraut, ketchup, or nothing, to suit their own tastes.

For a quick evening meal you can try frozen foods, most of which just require heating up in an oven. One of our favorites is frozen pizza, which has the advantage of allowing for personalized embellishment. You can add toppings like sausage, bacon, or just extra cheese, making an ordinary pizza into your own "special."

We recommend raw vegetables if your kids like snacks. Carrot sticks, slices of tomato, celery filled with peanut butter or cheese, and so forth. Dick likes to dish these out before dinner when his kids are really hungry. They go through a whole bowl of vegetables this way that they wouldn't even notice on the dinner table, which saves Dick from being the dinnertime vegetable ogre. David Vegetable Ogre uses the "you have to at least taste everything" approach. As a matter of fact, so does Dick when he forgets to put the raw stuff out ahead of time as usual, or when "what's good for you" is hot.

## Cooking for Your Kids

Easily prepared foods and the knowledge that you can always go to a fast-food place if you're stuck may give you enough breathing room to set up your own kitchen and begin the adventure of do-it-yourself food preparation.

Those of you who are familiar with making things in a home workshop (or who've taken a shop course in high school for that matter) will soon realize that cooking is a lot like any do-it-yourself project except that you get to eat the end product rather than sit on it. Just as you needed plans for a carpentry project, you'll need an instruction manual for cooking. And to carry the analogy a little further, you'll need tools and raw materials as well. The instruction manual for the kitchen is, of course, the cookbook. Kitchen equipment constitutes the tools, and groceries are your raw materials.

There are a couple of routes you can take to find a cookbook that best suits your own needs and skills. If money is no object we recommend you look through a variety of cookbooks at your local bookstore, selecting one that isn't too complicated and features basic recipes that have immediate appeal to you.

If you are on a tight budget, or you just like to research things before you buy them, we recommend that you consult your neighborhood library. Thumb through a number of cookbooks and check out the most promising so that you can try them out at home (recipes with buttery thumbprints on them may be good places to start). If you are satisfied with the results, buy the cookbooks of your choice in paperback if they are available.

Cookbooks that include basic instructions about equipment, meat selection, and the planning of recipes that go well together can be extremely helpful. Until you have established your own patterns it is often a puzzle knowing what to serve along with the pork chops or chicken you have selected to cook, and which things to start cooking first so everything is done on time. So any help along this line will probably be welcome. But don't get too discouraged if you find that these rather encyclopedic cookbooks offer more information than you can absorb. You'll probably want to rely on a few basic recipes at first anyway. If you can afford one of these books, use it as you would any reference book, to help you with specific problems in food preparation.

A gourmet cookbook might be fun to try some time so you can show off for your friends as well as your children. Cooking for kids is rewarding, but you need adult company as well, and it won't hurt to experience the pleasure of having your friends compliment you on your latest culinary project.

## Setting Up Your Kitchen

Just as the neophyte handyman would be more likely to start equipping a home workshop with a hammer and a handsaw rather than elegant routers and expensive planers, the beginning cook usually starts with basic kitchen equipment. Once you have the basic tools, new projects will suggest additional, special equipment. Eventually, you may find yourself taking great pride in your own collection of kitchen gadgets just as some people enjoy their sophisticated workshops. But buying even basic kitchen utensils can be a very satisfying and liberating experience in the beginning. In some sense it is a landmark of your increasing independence. One guy became absolutely ecstatic just thinking about having his own egg beater. He had owned an entire household of furniture before separation, but the kitchen stuff and the province it represented had not really belonged to him. An egg beater meant something very special. Of course, once he was actively established in his own kitchen, electric hand mixers and blenders, with their added style and ease, soon joined the liberation egg beater.

## The Kitchen Needs Chart

The Kitchen Needs Chart is designed for people without even a whisk to their name, to give you some idea of the things that are needed to start your kitchen, including some really ersatz implements that can get you going temporarily if you don't have the energy or time to start on your kitchen right away. You may even find a few items in the chart that you might be able to use when you know what you're doing in the kitchen.

| PERMANENT EQUIPMENT | TEMPORARY FILLER |
| --- | --- |
| frying pan | hub cap |
| sauce pan | empty coffee can |
| kettle | mess kit |
| large mixing bowl | empty paint bucket |
| spatula | paint stick |
| big spoon | ditto |
| big knife | fishing knife |
| small knife | ordinary jackknife |
| can opener | hammer and screwdriver |
| egg beater | fork |
| bottle opener | drawer handle or teeth |
| potato peeler | jackknife |
| colander or strainer | aluminum foil with holes |
| grater | jackknife again |
| kitchen timer | watch, biological clock |
| hot pads or oven mitts | wadded-up newspaper, sock |
| measuring cup | paper cup |
| measuring spoons | three fingers and thumb |
| cookie sheet or pizza pan | aluminum foil |
| canisters | original container |
| large plates | paper stuff |
| small plates | paper stuff |
| cereal or soup bowls | paper stuff |
| large glasses | the bottle, jelly jars |
| small glasses | paper cups |
| coffee mugs | plastic cups |

| PERMANENT EQUIPMENT | TEMPORARY FILLER |
|---|---|
| stainless steel forks, knives, spoons | fingers and jackknife |
| napkins | paper towels, jeans |
| table cloth | newspapers, shower curtain |
| dishwashing equipment | bathtub, shower, and soap |

You can prepare a great many things with this basic set of kitchen equipment (some of them even edible). You can also get along for quite a while with the temporary fillers, if somewhat brutishly. We know one person who made do with camping equipment and picnic plates for a couple of months before he got around to buying permanent stuff.

As for raw materials, basic cooking supplies will be built up over a period of time. You'll probably need such items as butter, sugar, salt and pepper, and so on, right away, but as you go along recipes will indicate other things to buy. And may we suggest, on the basis of hard-earned experience, don't buy spices because you "might need them someday" or because they look nice in the bottle. David still has a four-year-old bottle of bouquet of ragweed he doesn't know what to do with. Buy these things as you need them for a particular dish and in the smallest quantities possible. And try to use a shopping list. Writing your needs down will not only help you remember what to buy, it will also help protect you from buying impulsively.

## Main Courses

With pride and ignorance, we've prepared some recipes that have been kid-tested and approved and which might prove useful to other culinary neophytes like us. In most cases the recipes have the advantage of being relatively quick and easy to prepare, and we think that most of them are more or less foolproof, because we succeeded in making them. Anyway, you won't be able to screw them up too badly. They are generally flexible enough to be adapted to fit the tastes of most children. In some cases you'll be able to use them for more than one meal, which we find a terrific time-saving device. Finally, with a little creativity and more spices, you'll probably be able to make them palatable to your adult friends as well as your kids.

We've cooked these meals for our own and each other's kids.
They've liked them and we hope your kids will like them too.

### Koulack's Meat Sauce and Spaghetti

This dish is great. It's easy; it can be prepared before your kids
come over and it has a great deal of flexibility. My kids hate onions,
green peppers, and mushrooms, things I would normally include, but
they love ground beef and tomato sauce, so I go heavy on those
items.

> 2½ pounds ground beef
> 2 small cans of tomato sauce
> 2 small cans of tomato paste
> Oregano, salt, and pepper to taste
> 2 cups water

Cook the ground beef in a frying pan over a low flame, breaking
the meat up into little pieces and making sure that it all gets brown.
Drain the fat and combine the beef with the other ingredients and
cook over a very low heat. All this can be done several hours in advance and the sauce can be left simmering (not boiling) on the stove
with the top on the pot until mealtime. If your kids like onions,
mushrooms, or green peppers, chop them up into relatively small
pieces and throw them into the pot and let them cook all day.
I've found that I can actually get away with a few finely chopped
onions now, although my kids still pick out any mushrooms or
peppers they find and make vomiting sounds if they swallow a piece
of these horrible vegetables by accident.

This recipe feeds four for two days. Just reheat it the second day;
it tastes even better. If you want sauce with a little more flavoring for
adults, it's easy to make two pots, throwing vegetables and a little
garlic into the grownups' pot.

### Spaghetti

I still haven't mastered the art of putting in the right amount, but I
don't worry about it since I've discovered that I can use the leftover
spaghetti the next day. The first thing is not to believe that you need
a "four-quart" pot as it usually prescribes on the package. Just take
the biggest pot you have, fill it with water, throw in some salt, put on

the lid, and bring the water to a boil. When the water is boiling, ease in the spaghetti, a small bunch at a time so that the water continues to boil. When all the spaghetti is in, stir it around with a fork a bit to try to get the strands somewhat separated. Give the spaghetti eight to ten minutes to cook. You can taste a strand to see if it's done or if you want to have some fun, you and your kids can throw a strand against the kitchen wall. If it sticks, the spaghetti is done. Pour the water out of the pot, making sure the spaghetti doesn't fall into the sink. A strainer of some sort is helpful here. Rinse the spaghetti quickly under cold water to stop it from cooking, then throw it back into the original pot over a very low heat. And now for the secret. Put in some gobs of butter and swish the spaghetti around until the butter is melted over the strands. Your kids will love it.

Incidentally, if the spaghetti falls into the sink, rinse it and continue as if nothing has happened. To revitalize leftover spaghetti the next day when you are cooking a new batch, place the cold spaghetti in the strainer and pour the new spaghetti and boiling water over it. Then proceed as before with the combined batch.

### Koulack's Garlic Bread

For some reason, my kids love garlic bread. It's easy to make, tastes great, and adults like it, too. Leftovers can be reheated and eaten the next day.

*½ loaf of French or Italian bread*
*Garlic powder*
*Butter*

Let the butter stand for a while at room temperature until it's soft. Season to taste with garlic powder. We happen to like a lot of it. Slice across the bread from one end to the other leaving each slice attached to the whole by a thin strand of crust. It really doesn't matter if you cut all the way through; it's just easier to manage if you don't. Liberally smear both sides of each slice of bread with the garlic butter. Wrap in tin foil and place in an oven that's been preheated to 300–325 degrees. Let bake for an hour or so. If you want to leave it longer, just lower the temperature after the hour is up, and if you're in a hurry, you can bake it faster at a slightly higher temperature.

### Koulack's Hamburgers and French Fries

As you've probably discovered, there's nothing quite like hamburgers and french fries to satisfy the adolescent palate. But what you might not know is how easy they are to make.

### Hamburgers

*½ cup of cream of wheat*
*2 pounds of ground beef*
*1 egg*
*Salt and pepper*

Mix the cream of wheat, meat, egg (sans shell), salt, and pepper to taste. We find using one's hands the easiest way to get this chore done, but watch your pants. Divide into eight patties and put four in the fridge for the next day.

To broil in the oven, place very near the heating element for about a minute and then move the rack down a notch for about five minutes more. By the way, remember to keep the oven door open a notch when broiling. Then turn the hamburger over and repeat. You can adjust your cooking time, depending on how well you like them done, but don't neglect the initial searing.

### French Fries

*4 medium-sized potatoes*
*Cooking oil*

Peel and wash the potatoes. Then slice them so that they look like french fries. Place in bowl with water to keep them from getting brown. Heat up the oil until a potato slice will sizzle in it, preferably in a pot, but a frying pan with high sides will do. Use just enough oil so that it will almost cover the potatoes when you put them in the pot. If you estimate incorrectly, don't worry, you can always add a little more oil and too much won't really hurt. Before you add the potato slices to the oil, drain them on paper towels. Slip the slices into the pot a few at a time, being careful not to splatter yourself with the sizzling oil. With a spatula or spoon, turn the potatoes every now and then so that they all get a chance to be near the bottom of the pot. Remove when they look brownish or the way you feel french fries ought to look. Put into a serving dish with paper towels and pat dry to get as much oil off as possible, or put them in a double paper bag and shake them around. But don't leave them in a closed bag or they'll get soggy. If you use this method, you can also put salt in the bag to salt them while you shake them.

The cooled oil can be poured into a jar and saved in your refrigerator for another time. If all the potatoes aren't eaten, Dick suggests refrying them in hot oil to revitalize them the next day.

### Gatley's Hamburger Variation

If you drink beer, add it to Koulack's basic hamburgers. Poke holes in the final mixture and pour an ounce or two of beer over it and knead it in. Aside from the great flavor, it makes for moist, juicier burgers, but if you or your kids don't like the idea of beer, milk or water will add juiciness.

Instead of cream of wheat, I put in wheat germ and whole soy protein if I have it. I also like to make the patties thickish and pan fry them on burners hot enough to sear at first, then immediately lower the heat to medium.

### Gatley's Chicken in a Basket

This is an old reliable. Chicken is still a pretty good food buy and kids seem to like it just about any way that you can think of cooking it. Use a large, cut-up chicken or two pounds of chicken parts. If you use parts, you can buy the ones that your kids like best. My kids need a five- or six-legged chicken.

> *Flour*
> *1 egg*
> *¼ cup milk*
> *2 or 3 cups cornflakes*
> *1 teaspoon Beau Monde*
> *½ teaspoon green onion or celery flakes*
> *Salt and pepper*
> *2 tablespoons butter*
> *1 large cut-up chicken or 2 pounds chicken parts*

Prepare ahead of time, and in this order: about one-quarter inch of flour covering the center of a dinner plate; egg and milk, mixed lightly together in a bowl large enough to hold a piece of chicken;

*g Care of Your Children*

s of problems that separated fathers encounter in
lren depend to a great extent on how old the kids
f separation. Although this book tends to focus on
ildren are in the broad, middle range from early to
ve fully appreciate the special problems presented by
lescents. For very different reasons, these children
the greatest challenges to fathering after separation.

*ts*

of your children is still an infant when you separate
up against it. The kinds of catch-up, seat-of-the-pants
can get you over the difficult initial stages of separation
ldren just don't work with babies. You can't take an in-
onald's for dinner, or send him out to play while you
need an incredible amount of care and attention, and
know how well you're doing by gurgling, grinning, or
ell. They're always hungry, or full of gas, or filling up di-
than anybody can wash them, and if they go to sleep it's
t you out of bed again before you've recovered from your

or your baby may look quite impossible at first, but all of
ssociated with raising a child from infancy can be per-
fathers quite as well as by mothers (with the exception of
ling, of course). Once you've learned the necessary skills,
some understanding and acceptance of the demands, caring
aby can be one of the most rewarding things you'll ever do.
also begin with you as you are, without memories or re-
ey can grow up with you as a father who is separated, ac-
our situation, whatever it is, without question. Nor will they
e the problems older children often have in accepting other
at have become part of your life.
tunately, you won't be able to see your children every day.

plastic bag. (Use the one your vegetables came in. Turn it inside out if the inside still has junk on it.) Put your cornflakes in the bag and crush them. Use a rolling pin, side of a large jar, the heel of your hands, your feet, or roll on the floor clutching it to your person. Double bag it if the cornflakes start leaking out splits in the bag, or use two sheets of wax paper to do the original crushing, sandwiching the flakes between them. Dump the following things in the bag and shake it up: Beau Monde (a Spice Islands specialty), onion or celery flakes, and salt and pepper. Don't forget the cornflake crumbs if you did them in wax paper.

Set your oven between 350 and 375 degrees and let the butter melt in a small pan on low heat. Remove pan from heat and set aside. Wash the chicken under cold water and dry on paper towels. Then roll the chicken pieces in the flour to coat them lightly. Dip each one in the egg and milk mixture, allowing the excess to drip off, and then drop it in the bag and shake to cover the whole piece.

Lay the pieces on a greased cookie sheet or pan. Pour the melted butter over each piece and then put the pan in the oven for about an hour, or until a fork will go into a piece with ease. Undercooking is more of a problem with chicken than overcooking, so if you're in doubt, leave it in a little longer. Serve the chicken in a wicker basket or a bowl lined with paper towels.

My kids love the chicken with corn on the cob when it's in season. Just boil the ears in salted water (enough to cover the corn) for about seven minutes, and serve with butter and salt. Boil-in-the-bag corn or canned corn with butter is fine with them in the off-season. They also like raw vegetables with this meal, or tomato slices with mayonnaise.

When I'm lazy or I just want a change, pork chops made with those ready-made shaker bags seem to be accepted enthusiastically by my kids as a substitute for the chicken. You can also use Koulack's famous french fries instead of the corn if you like, too, giving variety to this basic meal.

### Gatley's Sukiyaki for Kids

This is really just a kind of stew, but if you stir fry it in a Chinese wok (cooking vessel) it's certainly a special one. A large frying pan will do just as well, the main trick being to do small batches at a time rather than one large one. That enables you to cook crisp vegetables rather than soggy ones. This meal is nice not only because you can often slip some vegetables into your kids' diet with style, but because it can be cooked even if you've forgotten to take your steak out of the freezer on time. The thin slices required are actually easier to cut when the meat is still a bit frozen.

> 1 pound sirloin or flank steak sliced very thinly in 2- to
>    3-inch strips
> 2 or 3 celery stalks
> 6 large white mushrooms
> 1 large onion
> 5 green onions
> 2 or 3 tablespoons peanut oil
> 3 slices ginger root
> 2 cloves garlic, chopped up
>
> SAUCE
> ⅓ cup soy sauce
> ¼ cup sherry
> 3 tablespoons sugar

A word about the soy sauce. Buy good stuff, Chinese if you can get it. It's sweeter than the Japanese kind and my kids seem to prefer it, but any good quality soy sauce will do. If the meat is not already frozen, put it in the freezer for about an hour to make it easier to slice thinly. Slice celery in small pieces at a very sharp angle, so they look like elongated letter "C's" on the ends. The mushrooms should be sliced lengthwise into little "T's," completing your alphabet. Just cut the onion into very thin slices. Green onions are slit down the middle and cut in half. Then you can combine the soy sauce, sherry, and sugar in a cup, and have all of these things standing by when you are ready to cook.

Heat the oil in a wok or frying pan. Add ginger root, if you've been able to find it, and a couple of chopped up cloves of garlic. When these flavorings are deeply browned discard them. Stir in some of the meat, cooking over a high heat until lightly browned, then add enough of the sauce for that batch, stir a few times, and throw in a portion of the rest of the ingredients. Stir until everything is covered with the sauce, then simmer for about five minutes on low heat, stirring now and then.

If you want you
broccoli, bamboo sh
detest. But experimen
will eat. I've found mi
covered with the sauce
ones in this way that the
Serve the sukiyaki wi
with easy-to-follow instr
ahead you can make reg
to cook. Try using a timer
and when to stop it.

One additional note befor
gearing all of your meals to
only boring, but very fattenin
we've described reassured us
cooking, and these experience
foods with less immediate app
easier on the fatty, fried foods
duce them to nutritious but '
things as chicken livers, fish, ar
afraid to become adventurous.
you.

*Takir*

The kind
raising their chil
are at the time
fathers whose ch
late childhood,
infants and ad
present some of

*Infan*

If one
you're really
methods that
with older ch
fant to McD
cook. Infants
only let you
crying like h
apers faster
only to rous
exhaustion.
Caring f
the tasks a
formed by
breast fee
and have
for your
Infants
grets. Th
cepting y
experien
adults th
Unfo

Thus involvement brings pain as well as satisfaction, because you will have to do your nurturing on a part-time basis. Seeing your young son or daughter for only a small portion of his or her earliest years may feel unbearable, and the press to know and be known by your child overwhelming. But whatever heartaches (or headaches) it may cause you, separation may offer an opportunity to care for your child which you might otherwise have missed. Many fathers who have become irrelevant bystanders after the birth of a child recover a vital role as separated fathers. As a consequence, there may be two adults on the job instead of one, each relieving the other in caring for the child. The more involved you become with the rigors of taking care of your child, the easier it will be to part with him when it's time for his mother to take over. So a feeling of virtue and fatigue may help to offset any sense of guilt or loss which part-time parenting may generate.

Having encouraged you to take part in caring for your infant, we ought to say a few things about how you can do it. First of all, if you don't know anything about taking care of babies or very young children you'd better get some help. Nowadays expectant mothers and fathers usually get their training in infant care from professionals. Almost every hospital that has a maternity ward offers courses in infant care and feeding you can attend, and you won't feel out of place, because prospective fathers often take these courses nowadays. They teach such basic skills as how to hold a baby, how to bathe it, change its diapers, and feed it, demonstrating how simple and relatively easy caring for your baby can be. They'll tell you about disposable diapers, premixed bottles of formula, and other things available now to make these tasks even easier. The confidence that this kind of course can give you will help to dispel some of the mystery and fear that often surrounds the whole process for both fathers and mothers, and will give you a good starting point for fathering your small children.

In addition to any courses you may take, friends and relatives may provide helpful suggestions and advice about caring for your child. Foremost among them, of course, will be the baby's mother, who'll probably want to be sure that you know what you're doing. Exchanges of information and advice with the baby's mother will be essential at this time for the infant's health and well-being and will remain important throughout the child's earliest years. Furthermore, it's a good idea if both of you maintain a close liaison with the child's pediatrician.

## Feeding Your Infant

The baby's pediatrician will undoubtedly have explicit recommendations about feeding your child. For example, solid foods are usually introduced one at a time to ascertain if your infant is allergic to one food or another. It is obviously essential that both parents exchange notes on the basis of the pediatrician's timetable for introducing certain foods, as to which foods the baby ate for the first time, when they were introduced, how your child liked them, and so on.

You'll also want to establish general guidelines for when you are going to feed the baby. We aren't sure if any one method is better than another, but it probably is a good idea for you to agree on some kind of timing. Most babies will adapt to whatever method you decide upon, whether it's feeding "on demand," "scientific" scheduling, or just feeding the baby when you both think humans "ought to" eat. Moreover, if your former wife is breast feeding the baby, since you can't offer this particular service, it's important that she introduce a "relief" bottle now and then, so that the child can become accustomed to bottle feeding. Otherwise, you'll be out of luck until the baby is on solid foods. We favor breast feeding if it's possible, but if your former wife is reluctant to include bottle feeding, you might point out some of its advantages. Training the baby to use a bottle will ultimately allow her some relief, not only when you have the baby, but at other times when she might want to leave the baby with a friend, or relative, or a baby-sitter, or even when she's just had it temporarily with breast feeding.

You'll probably find yourself a little timid and awkward the first time you try feeding your baby. This is par for the course for anybody, father or mother, separated or not. Babies are more rubbery than we are. They are sort of "floppy"; a baby's head doesn't seem to be stuck on very well, as if it might roll right off the infant's shoulders if you aren't careful. So you're *very* careful at first, and that's fine. Your self-consciousness will begin to fade and your confidence will grow when you notice the baby is quite oblivious to your awkwardness as you try to find a way of holding your child that is comfortable for both of you.

Holding the baby isn't the only awkward part of feeding him. Balancing him in one arm with his head propped against your chest, you then have to do all the rest of the work with one free hand, finding the bottle, testing it for temperature, popping the nipple into the baby's mouth, holding it while he guzzles his formula with gusto.

Unless you are a "pacer" who likes to keep walking with the baby, we've found bottle feeding a lot easier if you sit in a chair that has arms, a rocking chair perhaps, using one of the arms to help you prop the baby's head up so you don't become fatigued or cramped. A little soothing music thoughtfully turned on beforehand can really make the whole process beautiful, involving as it does such a special warmth and intimacy with another human being.

When your baby is done eating, she'll probably need to be burped. Held with her tummy on your chest and her head on your shoulder, a gentle massaging on her back, which presses her ever so slightly against you, will do the job as well as the traditional patting, producing audible burps or quiet sighs that assure sleep for both of you. If you don't burp your baby, chances are good she'll be crying with gas shortly after she's tucked in. If so, comforting and burping should have her nodding off again soon. Not to worry.

When you start putting solid food in the front end, things get less cozy and a lot more messy, including more solid and smelly stuff coming out the other end; so be prepared. If you weren't using disposable diapers before, you may want to start using them now.

In the earliest stages of spoon feeding, cover everything that cereal or liquefied green beans are likely to get on, including your baby, the chair and table, and the floor, not to mention yourself. Bibs are helpful, and so are high chairs which will hold your baby in place while you prepare the food and spoon it in—and back in. Be prepared to see a lot of it pushed out. Your baby is just beginning to develop the capacity to use his mouth for eating solid things, and naturally he won't be very good at it at first. Don't take it as a personal insult, or even necessarily a reflection on the food, though it will look and taste very unappetizing to you.

You'll probably find yourself having to reach into your bag of tricks to get your tot to open her mouth so you can feed her. Both of us have used various idiotic tricks, making airplane noises and funny faces while diving a food-filled spoon toward our child's laughing, open mouth. You may find yourself opening your own mouth like some kind of hopeful fish, ready to zip cereal into hers at the first opportunity.

Some babies develop a quick interest in feeding themselves, which it is well to encourage. If you have the patience to see your baby directing the odd spoonful of spinach at his forehead instead of his mouth, and you aren't too squeamish about milk being dribbled out of his cup, spoons falling to the floor, and glasses bounced off walls, you might find yourself out of the spoon-feeding business quicker than you thought. It won't be too soon.

## Things You'll Need

Being such unique little creatures, babies require some very special kinds of furniture and equipment, which their growth will make obsolete in no time. You needn't go broke seeing that your child has everything she needs. Friends may be glad to part with their old stuff. But if you don't know anyone with kids, you can easily obtain all the paraphernalia your baby will need from other parents anxious to get rid of the cribs and high chairs their children have outgrown. Laundromat and supermarket bulletin boards are always full of children's things for sale at reasonable prices.

Furthermore, you can probably do very well without some things, at least temporarily, especially if you haven't any room for them. Many people do without a bassinet for bathing their babies, washing their infants in the bathroom sink, for example. They make use of the laundry hamper or toilet top to hold the baby's fresh diaper and towel, her baby powder, ointment, or oil.

Similarly, makeshift cribs are standard equipment for most parents when they visit people who don't have kids. Chairs or pillows can be arranged to form barricades around adult-sized beds or couches to prevent the infant from falling out. If you're still worried, even though you know he can't climb out by himself, we suggest putting pillows on the floor for added safety.

We do think a baby carriage can be a good investment, if your baby doesn't come with one from his mom's. It will not only serve as a bed for a while, but will offer mobility as well, allowing you to get some exercise while your infant sleeps. You can visit friends, shop, or do the laundry, while the gentle, rocking motion of the carriage puts your baby to sleep.

High chairs are very useful, too. Your infant will stay put while you prepare his food, and it will support him while he is eating it. A high chair will save the rest of your furniture from encrustations of green plop and milk and allow you to look away if you can't bear seeing cereal dripping down his brow.

Baby blankets, waterproof sheets, extra sleepers, underclothing, diapers, and other items will also be needed to cope with the incontinent nature of your little kid. And when the baby's awake, rattles, small toys, and mobiles will keep him occupied and appropriately stimulated when you haven't time to play with him.

The pediatrician can tell you what kinds of vitamins, ointments, thermometers, vaporizers, and medications to have on hand for your child as well as how and when to use them. The baby's needs, and your own, will suggest other things and, of course, your communications with the baby's mother will keep you informed about special opportunities or requirements.

## Putting Your Baby to Bed

It may not seem like it to you, but babies sleep a disproportionately large amount of the time. The fact that they also wake up at odd hours when you wish they wouldn't doesn't detract from the pleasure of seeing them falling asleep. Content after their feeding, freshly diapered and dressed in their pajamas, children are incredibly captivating and vulnerable as they begin to drift off.

Putting your child to sleep for the night is often a very rewarding, very special time, as the labors and frustrations of caring for your baby gently give way to the warmth and closeness of your love.

David experienced these moments as luxurious and wonderful in the comfort of a rocking chair near the baby's bed, holding and rocking his child to sleep. Sometimes, when a rocking chair wasn't handy Dick created this delicious rocking motion by sitting on the nearest bed or sofa, rocking his body back and forth with his baby in his arms. This universal "rocking chair" can move in any direction you want, and it's a nice way of putting your child back to sleep, comforting both of you when she wakes up crying.

When you're ready to tuck your baby in and kiss him good night, he needn't be completely asleep as you tiptoe out of the room. He may even give a squawk or two, but usually he's just settling himself in. So don't rush back in (and really wake him up) when he makes these first noises or even cries a little, unless you want him to cry every time you put him down.

Many people give their children pacifiers to encourage them to sleep, possibly because they object to babies sucking their thumbs. Thumb sucking is natural. It comforts the baby, provides stimulation, and, unlike pacifiers, the thumb is always attached to the baby. It can't drop out of his mouth and get lost, waking him again just as he's dropping off. He can always find it even if he happens to wake up during the night. Dick used to plug his kids into a pacifier for an occasional breather; David didn't, but all of our children sucked their thumbs without any noticeable damage.

Like most kids, ours let go of the habit when it was no longer needed. Thumb sucking usually starts to fade out during the day, appearing only when your child is beginning to get tired, a nice indicator by the way that he needs a nap. Then later on it drops out at night as well. So we suggest you don't make a fuss about it. If your child persists in thumb sucking beyond "normal" time limits, his pediatrician will let you know if there's anything to worry about.

## Keeping Them Busy and Out of Mischief

There is probably no more difficult stage from the parent's viewpoint than the period when the child is just beginning to get around by herself. You have to be particularly alert at this time, keeping an eye on her to see that she isn't doing something that might injure her or creating havoc with your prized possessions.

One way of making things easier is to keep your child in sight and occupied while you are going about your business. Put a blanket on the floor where you're going to be working or reading, for example, and provide him with things that will keep him entertained. There are always things about that will do the job. Some of the most fascinating toys are found in your kitchen. Kids can play for hours with plastic cups, wooden spoons, and pots and pans.

But you can't count on kids to stay in one place indefinitely or rely on your own attention not to wander. There will be moments when your heart leaps because he's not where you left him. Reducing potential dangers will help to ease your mind. Make sure that anything that might cause your child harm is well out of reach or locked up. Medicines, razors, cleaning fluids, and the like, should be safely out of the way, even for a child who can climb. Remember, the most innocent things may be a source of danger for the curious child. We know one father, for instance, who had to rush his nosy kid to the hospital after he'd caught him having a snort of Daddy's after-shave lotion.

## Taking Care of Yourself

Taking care of a curious, always hungry, gaseous, upchucky, incontinent, completely dependent little human is an exhausting task that can become overwhelming if you don't take care of yourself. Although it is important for you to be able to accept the reality of these normal but extraordinary demands, if you are going to hang in there and retain your sanity, it is also urgent that you cope realistically with your own needs as well as the child's.

Try to arrange for a regular baby-sitter, someone in whom you have confidence, who can relieve you for a couple of hours during the day. Even if it only means getting away for a little while to take a walk by yourself or to drop in on a friend, it will give you some breathing space so that you can approach the rest of the day with your child refreshed and ready to enjoy his company.

Because you don't get to see your child every day you may feel a powerful pull to spend every moment of your time with her. But try to remember that it is high quality contact that children need. You can't provide warmth and affection if you're running around exhausted and angry. So don't feel guilty about taking a break when you need it. Don't get down on yourself, either, if you do get angry when you haven't had the sense or luck to take a break. Calm down and take the space you need to approach the problem constructively.

Raising kids is rewarding but it usually isn't easy. What's more some kids are harder for some parents to raise than others. Colicky, little pains in the neck, who never smile or burp on time, can make you look and feel rotten, while others enter this world with a smile, making it easy for you to feel like a "good" parent.

Luckily, most babies are so appealing that any gurgle or smile from them makes us feel good, miraculously offsetting the misery of their imperious and piercing cries for attention.

# Watching Them Grow

One of the things that makes little children rewarding is the pleasure of watching them grow. Funny-looking, little infants begin to develop into real people with their own personalities and capabilities. Because they are so incredibly dependent and demanding in their first months, it may seem as if they'll never grow up. Yet how quickly they begin to change.

These changes appear even more dramatic when you're separated. You may be dismayed by the amazing rapidity with which your child changes from one visit to another. As welcome as these changes are, they may also exaggerate feelings of being left out of your child's life. It's one reason why it is so important for you to keep in touch with the growth and development of your children when they aren't with you.

Keeping yourself in the know about your kids means having good communication with your former wife and anyone else who takes care of your children besides you. It's worth reiterating how important co-operative exchanges are to good parenting and personal satisfaction. If your little boy is ready to start on solid foods, or he's begun toilet training, both you and his mother need to know it. And if your daughter has learned how to stand up or to crawl, the other parent may appreciate hearing in time to make preparations for this sudden mobility.

Some of the better moments in your relationship with your former wife may be gifts of information about the children's development. Jeanette has grown her first tooth, or Tommy's lost his front one. Paul has started to learn the alphabet, and Sarah has grown two inches since her last birthday.

Your child's development can also be encouraged by timely memos about their emerging capabilities. Hearing that your son can now be trusted to climb trees without falling out of them may help you control your own anxiety enough to allow him to show off for you, and so on.

There are also some bumpy spots along the way when you can expect developmental problems as well as triumphs, and when you can use all the advice and information you can get. Experts like Dr. Spock can help you to keep abreast of your child's development, letting you know what to expect. It can be a great comfort to learn that something your child is going through is normal for his/her age and will pass, and a help to learn how best to lend a hand.

More immediately, it helps if separated parents have the courage to report developmental problems to each other when they occur in order to pool information and resources. One father took the plunge, for instance, by telling his ex-wife that he was having a problem with their four-year-old son, John. "He's wet the bed the first night here for the last three weeks, and I'm worried about him. Does it happen with you when he goes back? Because if it does, maybe we have to do something about the shifting back and forth or something. And if it's only happening at my place, I'd like to try to figure out what it's all about. Do you have any ideas? Has Johnny said anything about it to you?"

In another instance, tantrums were the problem reported. The mother of a rambunctious six-year-old compared notes with her former husband about the child's tantrums over getting dressed for school in the morning. The tantrums were soon short-circuited when she learned that her ex-husband managed to avoid the morning struggle by dealing with clothing decisions the night before when there was less time pressure on everyone.

Actually, it's fortunate if most of your child's problems are developmental and, by their very nature, pass. Even if you don't handle them as well as you'd like, you'll find that by the time you are finally ready to cope with a problem he's into something else. The resilience and adaptability of little kids, and their remarkable capacity to keep on growing in spite of practically anything, can make you downright humble.

This observation can help correct anxieties you may have about the effects of your separation on your kids. Whatever melancholy melodramas you may invent children often turn into comedies by their refusal to be typecast and their appalling negligence about following scripts. We don't want to slight Freud, but watching children grow makes for considerable optimism about the human capacity to overcome obstacles to growth. Kids grow in spite of everything.

It's lucky for us that they do. As kids get older, they also become less trouble to take care of. They do more things for themselves and they even begin to do some things for you and for the rest of the household, like washing dishes, mowing the lawn, and taking out the garbage. It's a delight when they begin to take responsibility for some of these things and a joy to see them become capable people.

They begin to entertain themselves and they develop more and more independent skills and interests, and before you know it they're not only growing up, they're growing away from you as well. Off they go to school, where other adults take over for you. More importantly, the world of other kids opens to them, and they begin to prefer the company of their peers to playing with papa.

The pride of seeing your children going to school or the joy of watching them playing with friends may bring you satisfaction as well as relief from having to spend so much of your time with them. It may also be accompanied by pain if they've grown faster than you were prepared for. Feeling left out or unwanted by your former playmates can hurt, until you get things back into perspective. So stop pouting. Your diminished importance to them only reflects your fall from all-star daddy perhaps to all-star dad, and represents their growth, not your shrinkage. But wait until they reach adolescence. Then things really get tough.

## Watching Them Go

Your first awareness of their approaching entrance into adolescence may come as a blow to you. Whereas your kid may have liked showing you off to his friends and bugged you to do things with them, suddenly you find yourself a social embarrassment. Your daughter's ashamed to be seen with you and cuts you dead if you run into her when she's with her friends. Your son may pretend he doesn't notice you, and is clearly embarrassed by your presence.

For separated fathers, already insecure about their relationship with their kids, this kind of behavior can be devastating. It is so easy to misinterpret this normal developmental phenomenon as final rejection. First relief often comes on discovering that you aren't the only one your kid is ashamed to be seen with. You may hear his mother catastrophizing about it, or other relatives complaining about your child's rejection of them. If they don't mention it, it may be out of embarrassment or politeness, so you may have to ask first. It helps to know you haven't been singled out. But even if you feel you have been, take into consideration what normally goes on with preteen-age kids.

On the threshold of adolescence, kids seem to become terribly conscious of themselves socially. They want to appear grown up and sophisticated to their peers, and the presence of a nurturing adult is mortifying. Even when you aren't actually patronizing to them, just being seen with a "parent" plunges them back into feeling like a child again, and experiencing a loss of face in the presence of their friends. For the time being, you are definitely not an asset. But you can be of help.

In spite of their apparent disregard for your feelings, kids generally experience a lot of guilt about being disloyal and disrespectful to you. They are in conflict between a healthy need to establish themselves in the world independent of you and their love and loyalty to you. They're depending on you to make the allowances, supporting their need to grow. Once you grasp the situation as a short-lived, developmental problem, you may be free to stop being hurt and to go back to fathering again, better prepared for adolescence proper.

### Teen-agers

Being a separated father of a teen-ager is a challenge. While on-going changes during this stage are not as clearly noticeable or as all-encompassing as they were when your child was an infant, they are nonetheless profound. The problems of fathering are also of a very different order, requiring letting your children go rather than holding them tightly to your bosom.

Their entrance into adolescence may first strike you when you notice the many social obligations your child suddenly seems to have, all of which exclude you. There are dances to go to, parties to attend, corner stores to hang out at, and so on. These plans are often made without consulting you at all, and sometimes coincide with visits when they are "supposed" to be with you.

One teen-age daughter we know regularly makes plans to meet a friend when she's visiting her father. Her father's house is much nearer to her friend's home than her mother's place so it seems perfectly logical to her to see her friend when she's at her father's. He feels hurt and confused by her apparent preference to be with her friend rather than with him. Having to compete with her friends for his daughter's time doesn't seem right to him.

It is at these times that being a separated father becomes particularly difficult. If his daughter lived with him all the time, he'd be glad to know she had friends. Even if it meant some loss of time with her, it would seem natural to him. He might even find it nice to get her out of the house for a change. But separated fathers often tend to grasp for every moment together.

If you're one of these grasping creatures, insist on her spending all of the time with you. Alternatively, sit around and mope a lot if you can't bring yourself to chain your son or daughter down. Of course, there's always a remote possibility that you might want to encourage your child to grow up.

As you might suspect, we see the last possibility as best for maintaining your sanity as well as your child's. The first two stances are plainly unproductive and well designed to make you either depressed or to alienate you from your child. But take heart. There are a lot of compensations if you decide to support your child's normal development.

On those rare evenings when your kids haven't any place to go and you do, you don't have to look for a baby-sitter. You'll no longer feel responsible for their having a good time when they're visiting you. You can all go about your own business without having to entertain each other. If you feel like doing something together you can, but you don't have to.

They'll be able to get around by themselves, so you won't have to ferry them to and from their mother's any more. They'll be able to drop in when they feel like it, not just during "visiting times." Even though they aren't home as much during official visits, you may actually see more of them from day to day than before. They may drop by to say hello or to pick up something, or because they want to ask your advice or to brag, or just because they feel like being with you sometimes. It's nice.

Furthermore, direct contact with them about things you feel are important suddenly becomes possible. While you may have had to go through their mother before when you wanted to talk about things like their schoolwork, now you can talk directly to them about it. When David's kids realized his interest, Joshua and Daniel began to call him whenever something important was happening for them at school. They would discuss strategy for studying with him, or stop by to show him the results of a test, or call up to talk about some project they'd been working on.

In other words, you may see less of them "officially," but your relationship with them becomes paradoxically more normal and less like that of a separated father. They are freer to take the initiative in making contact with you when they want to and you can respond to them more spontaneously instead of having to wait to get in your two cents at artificially scheduled times once or twice a week.

In essence, then, the trick is not to take your teen-agers' neglect of you personally, but to accept the necessity for them to go off exploring their exciting new world. They'll still be glad you're around.

This doesn't mean that you have to fade out entirely, or that you don't have needs or shouldn't make demands. On the contrary, like anybody else, teen-agers appreciate knowing you want to spend time with them. As far as we can see, there's nothing wrong with saying, "Look, I wish you wouldn't go out tonight. I was hoping we could go to the movies together." If it's still really important for them to go out, then wish them a good time. If you respect their needs at such times, it's more than likely they'll be willing to change their plans to accommodate your needs when it's important to you. After all, you may not be such a bad guy to be with sometimes.

# 4. Special Problems

Once you've become engaged in the intricacies of being a houseperson-parent, of taking care of your children, that is, you are bound to encounter a number of rather special problems. Some of these are ordinary enough, common to every family, yet special in the sense of being experienced as a problem or emergency. Tantrums and other disciplinary enigmas present us with especially novel and trying situations to solve, and when a child becomes ill we are similarly taxed to discover what to do.

Other problems are unique to divorced people with children, posing questions about how we can keep in touch with the children from whom we are separated, and how we are to cope with long distances or long absences from them. Birthdays and holidays, though "normal" as can be, also present extraordinary perplexities to the separated father. We hope our discussion of these issues will make the task of dealing with them easier and more effective.

There are several areas of importance to separated fathers that we haven't dealt with, some of them particularly sensitive ones, like fathering your children when you see them infrequently. Though we have touched on this particular topic in terms of communicating with your children "long distance" as well as in various other sections of the book, there are many aspects of this situation we know too little about.

We haven't dealt with fathers with rafts of kids either, though they surely have special problems—nor with some of the unique aspects of only children, or children from a new marriage. New marriages could be books in themselves, for that matter, but we hope we've touched on some of the issues that are relevant in our previous chapter on "new companions." In spite of these omissions, we have tried to deal with some of the more common problems that we know are bound to confound fathers who want to maintain a close relationship with their children. We hope your particular problems haven't been too badly neglected in what follows.

# When Your Kids Get Sick

## Infants

A big problem for parents, separated or not, is to distinguish between times when the noises or cries of their infants merely signify slight discomfort and times when they are indicative of greater distress. The main trick is not to panic. Basic common sense investigations will give you some idea of what to do.

If your baby cries it usually means she's wet, so see if a change of diapers is in order, and look for open safety pins while you're at it. If the baby is dry, he may be hungry; try feeding him if he hasn't had a bottle for a few hours. Between four and nine months of age, a bit of distress from teething may be responsible. So you might try giving your infant a teething ring or a hard bagel to chew on. And so on.

If none of these obvious solutions seem to work, check to see if your infant is running a fever, and if he is, you may want to call the doctor to see what he suggests. In fact, *any* time you're in doubt about your children, call your pediatrician. Don't be embarrassed to appear overanxious by calling him. Assuring worried parents is part of the pediatrician's job, and it's better to be reassured than distressed or sorry later. The baby's mother may have some helpful advice, too. You'll want to notify her in any case if it has been necessary to call the doctor.

## Older Kids

As your children get older and are able to describe their aches and pains, you'll have a better idea of what's serious and what can be treated with basic home remedies, like chicken soup and tender loving care. The most important thing to remember is that, generally speaking, kids are pretty resilient. They can bounce back from illness, bruises, and cuts fairly quickly; ailments that might lay you low, they'll shrug off with ease.

If your child complains of not feeling well, check his temperature. If he has a fever, give him aspirin or whatever his pediatrician recommends to bring the fever down, and start filling him with a lot of liquids. If his fever continues to rise get in touch with his doctor. To make him more comfortable you might sponge him with a cloth moistened with cool water or rubbing alcohol, taking care to keep him covered and warm, so he won't get chilled.

High fever or not, if he seems to have trouble breathing or complains of abdominal pain get in touch with his physician right away. And *don't* try to play doctor by administering medicines. You could make matters worse. While you probably shouldn't try to act as a diagnostician either, you can help the doctor to make a more accurate diagnosis by carefully observing all of your child's symptoms and describing them accurately. Does he just have a fever or is he vomiting too? Does she have a cough or a runny nose? Is she developing spots on her body; are her glands looking swollen, and so forth. As another aid to diagnosis and your peace of mind, try to keep abreast of any childhood diseases that may be going around, so you can be on the lookout for the first signs of it in your children.

Incidentally, it's a good idea to check with your own parents or records to see whether or not you have had any of the childhood diseases yourself. Dick couldn't remember whether he had had chicken pox or not so when both his children came down with the disease in quick succession, he spent several weeks checking himself for spots and feeling imaginary itches. He never came down with the disease, so we assume he'd probably had it. If you *haven't* had the particular infectious disease, you may want either to take preventive shots or to find some way to avoid your kids for a while. Getting childhood diseases when you're an adult is no fun, and the mumps are potentially dangerous for adult males in particular.

There are some basic things you should have in your (locked) medicine cabinet to take care of the minor aches, pains, and illnesses that your children will undoubtedly have. Thermometers are essential —rectal if your child is an infant and oral when your kid is able to hold the thermometer under her tongue for a minute or two. Keep several things in mind when taking your kids' temperatures: First, you usually don't have to keep the thermometer in their mouths for the two or three minutes recommended. Thermometers register temperatures fairly fast. Second, children's temperatures tend to fluctuate, so it's possible for a kid to feel fine even if he's a little off 98.6°. Third, the oral temperature is usually about a half a degree lower than the rectal temperature so when reporting to your doctor indicate how the temperature was taken.

In addition to the thermometer, you'll want to have aspirin (baby or regular strength, depending on the age of the child), adhesive bandages for small cuts, hydrogen peroxide or some kind of reasonably painless antiseptic and cotton for cleaning the cuts, and a packet of needles for removing splinters. Other items can be added as the need arises. When your child is actually sick, for instance, you'll probably have to pick up additional supplies and medication, according to the pediatrician's prescription. With these basic items, and a home medical adviser to guide you, you'll be able to take care of most of your kids' minor medical complaints.

# Socializing Your Children

## The Teaching of Personal Responsibility

We didn't like our original title for this chapter—*discipline*—because it connotes to us a rather one-way tyranny that is often passed off as a benefit to the child. Perhaps that just means we're hypocrites, afraid to call a spade a spade. But we hope our final choice of title more accurately reflects our emphasis on the importance of thinking about and planning what the child will learn as a result of our "disciplinary" actions.

Yelling at the kids or bribing them to shut up may be expedient, permitting you a necessary respite from madness, but your actions will also have profound and far-reaching effects on the kids. So, while we are *definitely* interested in tranquility and tidiness around the house, we also regard the ways in which we go about accomplishing these things with the kids of foremost importance, for our children and for ourselves.

Naturally, neither you nor we are likely to start out in the noble sense we're suggesting here. Most of us do *not* set out to "socialize" our kids, or specifically and consciously to teach them social skills and personal responsibility. In fact, as separated fathers we may be particularly reluctant to get into these areas because we know it may mean trouble for us with the kids that we don't want.

Consequently, we're likely to avoid confrontations at first, placating and "spoiling" our kids to keep the peace. But it's no use; we stand right smack in the middle of their normal development of power and autonomy. What *we* try to avoid, they'll run headlong into, "pushing" us to the point where we finally can't stand it any longer. Then *we* explode—and usually in the most primitive and un-socialized fashion. How embarrassing.

The main problem with playing "catch up"—of telling the kids what they should or shouldn't have done after they've done something to make you angry—is that it is ineffective. The sequence of events leading up to your anger may be understood by you (you may have bitten your tongue as you noted each step), but the kids will only be confused by your belated outburst.

Because of this, the pattern will tend to repeat itself over and over, which is even more infuriating: "I've told you a million times to . . ."; or, "This is the *last* time I'll tell you . . ." Oh, sure. But what these statements actually tell them is that you *expect* this behavior to continue in the future! And you have good reason to predict it, because what you are saying is *"When* you do it again, I'll punish you."* In your frustration you may then explain (and thus assure) the predictability of their behavior on the basis of certain rotten character traits: "You're irresponsible. You're too stupid to learn anything. You're just like your mother; your sister; your friends." It can get pretty ugly.

Fortunately, as pernicious as these patterns are, they can also be turned around constructively with forethought and planning, and hard work. But before we describe a few instances of what we mean by this, we'd like to point out another important feature of this process.

By observing the way you treat them, your kids will learn *your* ways of coping with and responding to conflicted and frustrating situations—a dismal thought, because you probably hate the way you handle things yourself. When you begin to see the kids acting the way you do, you may cringe. It may remind you not only of yourself, but of your own father or mother. You may feel like you're passing on the family curse to your children.

Becoming aware of the family monsters may be spooky and painful, and it may also be very helpful, if this insight brings about your resolve to do something about it. Exorcism in this case involves a shift from playing the catch-up disciplinarian (madman) to the role of guide and teacher to your children.

This doesn't mean you just switch brickbats to pencils, or that you need to become any less firm. Quite the contrary. It means planning things ahead of time, conceptualizing and articulating goals, conceiving means to accomplish them, and seeing if they work. It also means considerable "discipline" on your part to be able to carry all of these things out.

If you're about to grab your hairbrush and run—bear with us a little longer; it isn't as complicated as it sounds. Here's an example from our own experience:

When his kids used to troop into the house, slamming the door and throwing their clothes every which way, Dick often went berserk. He was furious with them for disturbing his peace, for not caring about who picked up after them, and he worried about how inconsiderate and sloppy and irresponsible this made them. But much of his alarm centered on the irrationality of his own "murderous" reaction. The situation repeated itself and he could see his belated rages were completely ineffective. What's more he felt this pattern was costing him the love and respect of his kids.

Fortunately for Dick, his woman companion just happened to be a behavioral expert, a psychologist with the training and knowledge to understand what was taking place and to recommend a more effective strategy. She suggested to her humanist (reluctant) companion that rather than his reacting with tantrums after the kids had dumped everything, he *teach* the kids how to enter a house!

Specifically, she recommended that he instruct the kids to rehearse the entire sequence of entering the house and to go through it with them patiently step by step. In this instance, it meant escorting the kids out of the house immediately after they came banging through the door, and telling them that he had something to show (teach) them. He then asked them to put their coats back on and to come in the house again as soon as he himself was inside, but this time to close the door behind them silently. Then they were to take off their coats and walk to the coat rack. Finally, they were to hang up their coats on the rack. It may sound ridiculous, but it was actually fun for all three of them. Even before Dick had completed the process, his son Rob had looked up brightly and said, "Oh, yeah, I get it!"

We don't guarantee results as immediate as this, especially if you tend to be very impulsive yourself, but one-trial learning of this sort isn't uncommon. The effects were also lasting in this instance; neither kid needed reminding again not to slam the door and it was very seldom that either forgot to hang up her/his coat again. More importantly, they had embarked on a new and happier course together, and were immeasurably pleased with themselves and each other; the kids with their newly acquired skills and Dick with the whole process. It also gave Dick a new respect for behaviorism by the way, and a greater willingness to listen to his new companion.

## Goals

Now that we've had our encouraging example, let's have a closer look at the process involved. Planning, we said, was preferable to reacting; this presupposes goals—that is, what it is we want to accomplish beyond having some peace and quiet around the house. First, let's elaborate a bit on what some of our goals might be for ourselves, then we'll talk about goals for the children.

One thing most of us can agree on is that we want to be *effective* as parents. It isn't just that we'd like to see our kids do as we tell them, although it might be nice to see them jump once in a while. We want to be able to help our children learn the skills and attitudes that will prepare them to live productively and comfortably in the world. We know the penalties they'll have to pay if they don't learn, and we know that because often we can see this when they do not, it is up to us to teach them what they need to know, though they won't always appreciate it.

The fact that our kids will frequently resist learning "how to behave" and how to take care of themselves brings up another of our goals and that is: how can we go about all these wonderful things in a way that still assures us a happy and enjoyable life with our kids? As separated fathers the last thing we want to do is to alienate our children. We're usually quite fearful to come down hard on our kids for fear that they won't want to see us, and that we'll look bad in comparison with the children's mother and perhaps because we may already feel guilty enough about "leaving" the kids. As long as we continue to feel vulnerable to our children's potential or imagined judgments about ourselves, we're going to have a hard time functioning as their parents.

We pull ourselves out of this hole by realizing that our kids are depending on us to behave normally, even though the situation is unusual. Paradoxically, when we're behaving like parents—feeling awful about disciplining them, the kids feel more reassured by our bossy authority. So, our needs coincide, oddly enough, when both of us are engaged in the normal processes of socialization!

That being the case, let's look at what our goals might be for the kids.

## *Goals for the Kids*

We believe one of the main things children (and adults) need to learn is personal responsibility. This isn't just a euphemism for obedience—an acquiescence to authority which merely reflects a continuation of dependence on others to tell you what to do. It means learning to become self-reliant—shifting from reliance upon external guidance and control to an internal and personal control. Rather than expecting others to see what needs doing, to initiate appropriate action and to keep reminding them about it, your children need to get to the point where they can do these things for themselves. These skills then become part of their repertoire.

The basic goal of personal responsibility underlies all of the more specific things we want our children to learn, not only things that pertain to taking care of themselves, but also all of the things that relate to ways of living with other people: consideration, respect for the rights of others, generosity, fairness—even love and caring. Once the child has learned the specific *ability to respond* with kindness, generosity, and so on, he then has the *response-ability* to behave in harmonious ways with the world, not as a duty, but because he has the *choice* of doing so. He can decide for himself whether or not he will practice the interpersonal skills he has learned. He can even choose to transcend his own immediate imperatives out of respect or love for others.

## *Means*

But our children learn (or fail to learn) these things from us, from the way we treat them. How are we to do it? As men just out of ruptured marriages, we may not feel we've transcended a hell of a lot ourselves. Nor have most of us been fully responsible for "socializing" the kids up to now.

These problems may be minuscule if you only have the kids for short periods of time; after all anyone can be on his best behavior for a day or two, and besides, you'll probably want everything to run smoothly anyway; but longer visits are different.

If the children are "yours" for extended periods and/or very frequently, you can't escape the many problems that will demand action on your part as a "disciplinarian." But along with this increase in problems, will also go an expansion of both opportunity and time to work on these problems with your kids—to take your part in helping your children to grow up okay.

In some instances, if for various reasons their mother is lax in certain areas, or if you are particularly qualified to teach them something, the kids may have to rely *entirely* upon you.

One of our clients discovered, for example, that his youngest daughter seldom took baths when she was at her mother's place. He noticed a rather horrendous odor emanating from her every time she walked in the house. Realizing that he couldn't control Amy's behavior when she was at her mother's, he began to make bathing a required part of the bedtime ritual at his house. To guide her he set up a calendar so that Amy could check off each night that she'd had a bath. He also reminded her personally about other aspects of basic hygiene for a while, like changing to clean clothes and brushing her teeth. He felt like quite a nag for a time, but his concern paid off; his daughter began to attend to herself, and not only at his house. Her mother began to comment on Amy's surprising interest in good grooming at her place too.

So there's a lot for us to do as fathers, even if few of us are experts in raising kids.

## Structure

After you've told a kid *what* you expect of him, you may need to tell him *how* to do it or provide him the structure for carrying it out effectively. In Amy's case, for example, her father afforded her the chance not only to keep clean—she already knew how to wash and brush her teeth—but also to keep track of her own behavior with the calendar—to experience control of her own destiny by checking off *for herself* each successful task. In time, with her father's consistent encouragement, her behavior became so habitual that it tended to run itself off unaided; it now *belonged* to Amy completely.

This example illustrates another beneficial feature: generalization of the newly acquired skills to other places and situations. Once Amy became personally responsible for her grooming—once she "owned" it in other words—she began to practice taking care of herself at her mother's as well. The implicit compliments he received from Amy's mother about it were an important side-benefit of this for her separated father. This helped him to feel more confident of his ex-wife's view of him as a father, because, although he was concerned that it might stimulate competitive reactions in his former wife, it actually seemed to smooth out some of his interactions with her.

The use of deadlines is another example of structure: The children's rooms in Dick's place were a no-man's land and a constant source of frustration for him and for them, because no matter how often he told them to pick their things up, he always found everything in a mess next time. In the summer months when they were there every day, it became even worse. Setting a noon deadline for their rooms to be tidied and holding absolutely firm about it brought about a change almost overnight. But structure alone in this and in most instances is not enough. There have to be some consequences contingent on satisfactory performance. In this case, the children lost television privileges for the evening if their rooms flunked inspection. Although they weren't actually that interested in TV during the summer, it worked. The oldest got things right without missing a single night's privileges, and even decided to throw in a vacuuming once in a while. After one rare but very noisy tantrum that took her voice away for a while, the little squirt came around too.

## Communicating Your Purpose

Most of us need incentives of some sort to encourage us to do things in spite of our inertia, especially if there are competing needs operating. So we can hardly expect high ideals to serve as motivating principles for our children. Nonetheless, if your reasons for expecting them to behave in certain ways are based on foresight rather than expediency, and if you have some broader, long-range reasons for disciplining them, don't keep it a secret. Tell them. You needn't expect a commendation; they'll probably think what you're saying is crap, especially if you bully them with it; but they'll still grasp the idea that you have *something* in mind. If you keep your explanation simple and concrete they may even begin to catch on.

## Incentives

We won't attempt to catalogue the countless ways in which parents have attempted to reward and punish their children over the years. But we do have some general comments.

On the whole we much prefer to reward our children than to punish them, not only because we like our kids and we want them to like us, but also because rewarding them *works* better—with respect to all of our goals with our children. Punishment, on the other hand, often seems to create more problems than it solves, especially if it isn't well conceived. It may fail to make clear *what* is being punished as well as neglecting to point the way to more desirable behavior. It also teaches the child how to punish other people, so you need to think twice about using it.

Rewards are definitely on the plus side with respect to all of these deficiencies. Some are healthier and more effective than others, in terms of our over-all goals. Recognition and praise for personal accomplishment are particularly good ones to use, for example, with or without additional goodies, and they don't rot your children's teeth. The awarding of greater personal freedom and trust may also be well-earned rewards and welcome additions to both of you. Bedtime stories and trips to the zoo educate as well as reward and may be better incentives in the long run than straight cash or candy.

With a little imagination it's usually possible to make incentives constructive even when you must use some form of punishment. Reduction of television viewing, with all its violence, might have had a salubrious effect on Dick's children, for instance, although we may never know. Withdrawal of cavity-encouraging sweets is another example, and even a precipitous trip to bed may do a tired child some real good.

Coping with tantrums is particularly trying to parents, but when you isolate a screaming child until she cools down, you can also structure the situation so that the child actually has an opportunity to accomplish something—control. She may be told, for example, that she can come out *when she is ready*—that is, when she has calmed down and is prepared to be reasonable with other people—thus shifting her from doing battle with you personally to learning control over her own emotions. You can even greet her success with praise when she reappears, because you will now have something worth while to reward instead of something to punish.

Circumstances don't always allow us to do things the way we would like to, however. There are occasions when we simply don't have the time and patience to respond constructively to our children's behavior—when it's either a choice of spanking the kids or allowing them to do something we don't want them to.

There are times, for example, when our children need to engage in testing the limits of what they can "get away with," as well as testing our resolve to enforce these boundaries. If we're to be effective as parents we have to be firm at these times. The kids need to know where they stand with us and that we mean what we say. A great deal more trouble and confusion accrue from being wishy-washy than from being firm at these times.

It's customary for kids to test these things out when you're not emotionally and mentally in the best shape to be constructive, and when there are other people around to apply social pressure on you to avoid making a scene. You may have to risk appearing like an ogre in the supermarket if you want to cut a child's behavior short.

In using physical punishment—spanking on the bottom only that is —you still need to know what you're doing, especially if you're angry with the child. The purpose must always be ultimately constructive even if the methods are punishing. This means practicing restraint and moderation—one spank with an open hand is often all that's needed. There is nothing necessarily wrong if you experience some relief and satisfaction from spanking your kid occasionally; it's only human, but it had better be only a fringe benefit and not your main purpose. Some of us can get to feeling pretty angry with our children at times—when the pressures and frustrations of raising children reach really egregious proportions—but we need to find other ways of releasing this energy. You may recall, for instance, some of our suggestions for dealing with anger toward your former wife, such as taking your anger for a walk somewhere where it can't do you or anyone else any harm.

But don't take a walk every time just because you feel bad about having to discipline your children. Don't duck it if you need to take a strong stand with your kids sometimes, because if you do you may *really* foul up your relationship with your children. As one of our clients described it: "My dad was afraid to hurt me. He was very strong and when he hit me one time I sailed clear across the room. I made such a terrible scene about it that he thought he'd practically killed me—and he never laid a hand on me again. I never expected him to quit like that. And we've never seemed close to each other since then."

So hang in there with your kids, even if you hate feeling like a "bad guy." They need you, and they need to be able to count on your guidance.

One last thing is worth adding as a special caution for separated fathers. We definitely think you should *not* fool around with your time with the kids as a form of reward or punishment. Never make seeing the kids contingent on their being good or bad—the potential damage is too great. Don't threaten them by telling them you won't see them however rotten they may have been, and if you even suspect that they're worried that you might do so, reassure them that it isn't true.

You're trying to establish a new life for yourselves together—so you don't want to go threatening anyone with abandonment or neglect even if you do feel miserable and angry with them at times.

## *Follow Up*

Once you've run through one of these sequences we've been talking about, whether it's a spanking or an elaborate training program in hygiene or tidiness, it's a good idea to follow it up—observing its results and discussing them with the kids afterward. This may be your opportunity to give them a hug and renew feelings of love, or a chance to learn what's happened and how it worked. Frequently it's the most rewarding part of the whole process.

In the case of the messy rooms, for instance, when Dick was talking over the results of the project with his kids, he suddenly noticed an unexpected yet predictable bonus: "Have you kids noticed? I don't scream and yell at you guys when I come up here any more! I don't even notice your stuff lying around and anyway it doesn't matter; I know it'll all be cleaned up tomorrow. Boy, is that nice." His kids had to agree.

# Keeping in Touch with Your Kids—Phoning and Letter Writing

## Local Calls

Although you may see your children frequently, it's a good idea to phone them from time to time—just to see what's new and to tell them what's happening with you. If your kids are small fries though, don't count on snappy conversation; they're not apt to talk very well on the telephone. Even so, little kids do need frequent contact and will feel left out if you don't say hello when you call up their older brother or sister. Brief and primitive as it may be, a chat with the small ones can be a nice way to keep in contact.

It's also useful to remember that very young children are not only inarticulate on the phone, but they generally have a short attention span as well. Therefore, you can expect big pauses or silences at the other end of the line; but these shouldn't be taken as a sign of rejection. All it means is that your child has run out of things to say and would probably like to get back to whatever he was doing when you called—not that your child doesn't love you any more. Children's needs for contact are also more basic and simple than ours; a short hello may be all they need to feel in touch and loved by you. They can't help it if you're more complicated. Older kids are somewhat more like us and telephone calls can play other important functions for them. Besides maintaining basic contact, phone calls can serve to communicate information and interest in what the children are doing. One father we know, for example, makes it his business to find out when tests are coming up or projects due, and phones his children to ask how they're doing in their studies and on exams. In this way he's not only able to transmit his values on education regularly, but he's also able to make helpful and timely suggestions over the phone when one or the other of his children is bogged down in his studies.

Another side benefit of frequent phone contacts is that it keeps you up to date on events you may want to attend. For example, when David's kids were playing hockey, game times were irregularly scheduled, and often decided upon only a few days in advance. Telephone contact gave David the opportunity to stand outside in forty-below Winnipeg winters, freezing his ass off while he cheered his sons on to greater feats of brilliance on the ice.

## Telephone Phobia

Phone calls can also help *you* to feel better, especially when you're missing the kids. It's easy to get down in the dumps or feel guilty if you haven't seen them for a while, even for a few days, and a call can be an enormous relief. But some dads aren't much better than small fries on the telephone. They have a personal dislike for this form of disembodied contact; they're not very good at it, and they may have to force themselves to dial the number.

Others avoid telephoning their kids because they're afraid their children will make demands that they can't or don't want to meet, such as picking the kids up "right now, Daddy" or coming to the party at Mommy's house. Separated fathers may be reluctant to commit themselves to any number of contacts that *may* be requested by their children, feeling badly about doing so despite good reasons to refuse. Lacking the courage to say *no,* these fathers may avoid giving their kids any chance to ask for anything. Happily, with practice, these same fathers generally learn to feel more comfortable refusing their children's requests, especially when they come to realize that the kids won't fall apart when they're denied something. The initial discomfort dissipates and it soon becomes a pleasure to hear the voices of their kids on the other end of the line.

## The "Operator"

One person's voice that usually isn't welcome when a separated father calls is that of his ex-wife. Just the sound of it may arouse feelings far afield from what he intended to experience when he called. It isn't uncommon for the children's mother to take advantage of the opportunity to bend her former spouse's ear about a whole panorama of issues and items he'd sooner not hear about. Yet, this seldom dissuades anyone from ringing up his kids. In fact, after their initial awkwardness with each other, both parents will probably welcome these occasions to bring each other up to date on the kids. If you haven't reached that point yet, or if you're pessimistic that it will ever occur, persist—don't let difficulties with their mother, which are probably temporary anyway, interfere with your contact with your kids.

Incidentally, because parents often tend to speak *for* their offspring about a variety of things, you may want to insist on hearing about your children's experiences firsthand. Don't be satisfied with just your parent-to-parent chats about the kids, even though they may be invaluable most of the time.

## Long Distance

Obviously, when you live far from your kids, phone calls and letter writing become even more important. The telephone is the better bet, because it's person-to-person, so to speak, rather than one way. But long distance calls are expensive. They're also terribly disappointing if your kids aren't in when you call. One way of reducing missed telephone calls and cutting costs is to try to call your children at approximately the same time each week, or however often you call —preferably on a Sunday or early in the morning when the phone rates are cheapest. A consistent time will give you more assurance of catching your kids in, saving you disappointment and allowing you to feel comfortable about making a station-to-station call.

As far as letter writing is concerned, we recommend frequent, short notes telling your kids what you're up to and asking about things that they're doing. If a tendency to long letters limits your production, get cards or anything else that has limited space for your messages; you'll feel good about sending these shorter notes, and your productivity will increase.

If your kids are fairly young, send them a batch of stamped, self-addressed envelopes to make it easier for them to get a letter off to you. Fancy stationery with their names printed on it might be an added inducement to pick up a pen and to get a letter off to you. But if they don't write very often, try not to be upset—they still love you; it's just that few kids get the hang of expressing it by writing letters.

If you feel you aren't getting enough action through the mail, perhaps it's time to get on the telephone.

## Tapes, Photos, and Things

With a plentiful supply of tape recording and playback machines available, you may want to add the personal touch to your mail. Even though it probably won't last long, the novelty of these gadgets should bring you some nice returns for a while when you send one off to your kids.

Other things can liven up the mails too: Photographs, and drawings (encourage the nonverbal little people to send you *their* productions; they'll love it), relevant newspaper clippings, and cartoons and jokes—anything you can think of that's personal and informative and fun.

## When You're Traveling

If you're off on vacation without the kids or traveling for any other reason, send post cards. The pictures on the cards are likely to tell your kids more about where you are than your words—and your added description will only have to fill them in about the details of what you're doing. Post cards are shorter and easier to write than letters, so they're better for keeping up your contacts with the kids. Letters often go unappreciated by youngsters anyway, even if they can read. What they want is a quick contact and a touch of news, and that's all. They may spare themselves the details you went to so much trouble to write.

If you want some mail in return, be sure to leave an itinerary with dates and places and prestamped envelopes addressed to the places you'll be stopping. If you also pencil a deadline date on each envelope when it has to be mailed in order to reach you, you're more likely to get it on the road rather than at home, later.

Again, if you don't get mail, it doesn't mean their affection for you has waned—more likely it's a sign of a poor postal service, or whatever rationalization you prefer to cover the fact that kids just aren't champion letter writers. Besides, if you're fussing about mail from home, your trip must be pretty dull anyway.

# Long Trips or Absences from Your Children

Paradoxically enough, fathers who see their children frequently often experience difficulty in coping with prolonged periods of separation from their kids. This is especially true if the absences are a matter of choice on the part of the father.

One father we know had an opportunity to spend his summer vacation on a fishing trip with some old friends. After a lot of soul-searching he decided to go on the trip even though it meant not seeing his kids for a month. He didn't enjoy the trip. He spent most of the time feeling guilty about deserting his kids and worried that they wouldn't love him when he returned. Naturally, his fears were unrealistic; the kids had a great time while he was gone. But *his* vacation had been ruined.

This kind of situation is all too common. Many fathers feel they should spend every available moment with their kids. But to deny yourself some fun in life consistently may be asking for trouble, generating more difficulty in your interactions with your children than going ahead with your plans. If you don't take the opportunity to revitalize yourself, you may begin to resent your children, finding them a burden instead of a joy.

More often than not, your children will understand your absence and encourage you to enjoy yourself, even though they might miss you. Just as they would seize the opportunity themselves to go to camp or to spend time with their friends if they had the chance, they'll understand your desire to do the same thing. What they will expect from you in return, perhaps, is an occasional phone call and some post cards and letters to let them know you're thinking of them. They'll probably get a kick out of these previews of your adventures and will have something to look forward to when you get back. It's a good idea to take some pictures to spice up your narrative later when you give them the blow-by-blow description of your trip. Incidentally, not to plug any particular product, but if you use instant-developing film you can actually send them a piece of your trip while you're still on it.

Before we fade off into the sunset, a few additional comments. It would be erroneous to leave you with the impression that all separated fathers feel obliged to suffer when they're absent from their children for a while. Parting may be sad or even anxiety-provoking as you "flee," but you may find yourself whistling a little farther down the road. Away from all the familiar reminders—the places and faces and routines—in new surroundings, you *can* forget to feel guilty or worried and enjoy life as you find it.

After a reasonable period of time, if you are still overwhelmed by guilt, perhaps you had better return, or telephone to validate or disconfirm your anxieties. It may be preferable to throwing away your time and money or to allowing your fantasies to grow unchecked.

But if this idea sounds overly dramatic and ridiculous when you think about it, then what you have been doing is catastrophizing again. If you want to indulge yourself in this way, *olé,* but since you've gone to so much trouble to get away, you may decide to enjoy yourself as planned instead.

"Forgetting" about your kids and enjoying yourself isn't disloyal or uncaring any more than your children are disloyal to you if they have a good time while you're gone. *They* certainly won't berate themselves for it—would you? If you miss each other a little, or even a lot, and it's love that bubbles up from thoughts of them instead of guilt— great. You've found the perfect moment to write them a post card or to telephone to tell them you love them. By celebrating your thoughts of them in this way, you'll let go of them happily, ready to return again to your new adventures.

# Birthdays and Holidays

In addition to fun and games, special occasions often mean special *problems* for most separated fathers. Aside from the usual difficulties that birthdays and holidays present to any parent, two uniquely different kinds of dilemmas arise for fathers who are divorced or separated: birthdays and other occasions of *short* duration, such as Christmas Day, tax us with how we are to share this limited and presumably precious time with our children, with the children's mother. On the other side of precious are the conundrums and difficulties of coping with having the children all to yourself for *extended* periods during the holidays—on Easter or Christmas week, or for a whole summer. Both are problems of a "special" nature, which demand extraordinary planning and preparation if these two different kinds of opportunity to be with your children are to run smoothly and be rewarding.

## Red-letter Days

Many festive occasions you'll want to celebrate with your children won't fall on days when they are scheduled to be with you. Some separation agreements try to anticipate this difficulty by making specific provisions for partial visitation on each child's birthday; the father is usually entitled to see his child for an hour or two on this special day. But there are seldom such highly specific provisions for Christmas, Chanukah, or other holidays that a family might normally expect to celebrate together; and it's probably just as well. Partial visitation provisions of this sort are really quite inadequate at best.

In trying to be fair, the authors of such agreements fail to appreciate that the purpose of these occasions is to celebrate and enjoy each other, not to award parents precise pieces of a duty, obligation, or prize. In any event, in the actual living of them, these arrangements are seldom likely to be experienced as fair. They fail to appreciate how a token couple of hours can exacerbate rather than assuage feelings of unfairness and discrimination. And more importantly, it's patently obvious that nobody can possibly get into the proper spirit of the thing if he has to watch the clock. There are much better ways of handling the situation which are far more satisfying for everyone concerned.

If you must divide up a birthday or any other special day because you'd both like to be with the kids on the "right" day, we'd recommend that you split up the time fairly equally and plan it so that each half is part of a somewhat larger chunk of time with the kids, so that you won't be rushed and will all have enough time to do the things you'd like. You might actually hold the celebration the night before, for example, keeping them overnight so that you can enjoy the morning of the big day with them. Their mother will then have the afternoon and evening with the kids all to herself.

Turn it around if you like, especially if the children's mother and you prefer to alternate who will throw the afternoon party (to which other children are more likely to be invited) and who gets to see the kids first thing Christmas or birthday morning. Real fairness can come about through this kind of sharing of the unique features associated with birthdays and other holidays.

But we've found that it isn't really necessary to observe these red-letter days on precisely the right date in order to enjoy them with our kids. In fact, it's David's policy to start the festivities in advance by celebrating the event on the first regular visiting day closest to the occasion. When you think of it, this isn't really such a radical departure from what goes on in most families. Parents often decide to hold a child's birthday party on the nearest weekend to give them ample time to prepare for a horde of kids.

It needn't be the child's gala occasion that's honored at a more convenient time for everyone, either. Dick's kids had a great time recently helping their dad celebrate Father's Day, thinking their befuddled father knew what he was talking about when he said it fell on June 12 in Canada, which happened to be on his visitation schedule. They all had a good laugh later when they discovered his error, because it didn't matter at all: they had all had a wonderful time. As a matter of fact, it turned out very well, because Father's Day actually fell on an *off* weekend when Dick planned to be out of town.

David generally makes it a rule to celebrate his own birthday on the nearest *Saturday* night, by taking Joshua and Daniel out to eat.

In this way the occasion is made even more special, particularly because David doesn't have to cook or do the dishes, which seems appropriate, and leaves him more time to spend with his kids.

The children certainly have it made however you arrange to celebrate these events, especially birthdays. They'll have two birthdays of their own rather than one to enjoy, and don't think they don't know it. With their own as well as everyone else's to celebrate, the kids may also come to expect a whole round of birthdays stretching across the entire year! One little kid began to ask, "Where's my present?" every time she came over. So, if anything, you may have to be careful about "spoiling" the kids with all these festivities.

As these events become a little less precious, things will also begin to loosen up in your negotiations with your ex-wife about birthdays and such; it may even become kind of amusing. Instead of competing for the privilege of hosting the main party, for example, you may actually start jockeying to see which one of you will have to throw the big shindig for all the neighborhood kids! Certainly, with time and lots of contact with your children, these things needn't stimulate the anxiety and urgency for success they often do early on.

## *"Winning" the Honors*

If you've won (or lost) the toss to see who'll do the honors on the children's birthday, you may find that running a birthday party for kids isn't as simple as you might think—or as impossible. If your kids intend to invite their friends you're likely to have hordes of screaming, hungry children running around the place. If you can tolerate noise and roughhousing, you'll probably survive. But if you can't, there are some alternatives to ruptured eardrums and aspirin.

One thing you can do is hold the party outdoors—if you're lucky enough to have warm, clear weather. Contingency plans in case you aren't so lucky will also serve for winter birthdays, and can still give some measure of relief. Taking the kids bowling or swimming at the local pool will give you a little elbow room, and a movie matinee or a visit to the local museum or planetarium may keep them quiet—you hope.

If you feel that taking care of a great horde of youngsters is too much for you, however, don't be afraid to enlist the aid of a few of the guests' parents. They'll generally be quite sympathetic and glad to help. On the other hand, if you aren't a social butterfly and you don't really know the parents of your children's friends, don't sweat it; if you feel like turning thumbs down on hosting the whole gang, so be it. Reduce the party to a size with which you'll feel comfortable. One encouraging experience with a few guests may lead to bigger and better things later on.

If it's just feeding these masses of piranhas you're concerned about, there are a number of possibilities. Big pots of spaghetti and meat sauce, or hamburgers, hot dogs, and french fries are sure-fire hits if they're within your capacity, along with the traditional cake, ice cream, and soft drinks, of course. But if even the idea of cooking for so many kids turns you off, there are lots of well-known prepared-food places that specialize in bailing parents out. It might be more expensive, but it saves a hell of a lot of work.

## Private Parties

If your kids have already invited their friends to their mother's for a birthday party, or you've decided you don't want any part of a big bash, a private party will probably be much more to your liking anyway. It's potentially so much more warm and intimate than a big marathon event. But whichever you choose, make sure you arrange it so that you'll be able to share in the enjoyment of the celebration; don't get stuck in the kitchen or tied up as a social director while all the fun and action are taking place elsewhere.

## Home for the Holidays

Holidays like Easter, Christmas week, and summer vacations mean coping with the responsibility of having the kids full time for extended periods. This may be more of a problem for fathers who aren't used to having the kids a great deal already, especially those who *only* see their kids at these times. But the long school holidays create special difficulties for any single parent, however often they see their children.

Chiefly, the difficulties are of two general kinds: how to find the time to be with the kids over the holidays (or to cover the time when you can't), and how to spend it with them.

## How to Find the Time

For people with flexible work schedules like ourselves there are usually few basic problems in arranging to spend time with the children over the holidays. But fathers with fixed work hours and fairly short vacations are faced with a number of difficult choices and problems. They will have to make arrangements for child care or baby-sitters during working hours if they can't make this time available. If so, it may still be possible to spend some time with the kids by taking an afternoon off, or having lunch with them. And it may be a good time to bring them to work with you occasionally. Perhaps you might even be able to take some of your work home with you.

Of course, various events and festivities that usually take place during these holiday periods will keep your children busy and entertained, and should also free up a few days to spend with them. You may not get a whole week or two off the way they do, but you should get *some* time to celebrate.

Merely breaking loose from work won't solve all your problems, however. Even if you *do* have some vacation time, it isn't likely to be free from competition. Other people besides your kids may want to enjoy some time with you, like your new companion, or your friends, and you'll have to dicker with them about it. Among those who will cherish the thought of your having some time free is yourself. But vacations with the children seldom live up to their promise as "interludes of recreation and rest."

## How to Spend the Time

Consequently, you'll be at odds with yourself to some degree thinking about how you would like to spend your vacation. It will help in the long run if you decide ahead of time what you are prepared to give up in order to be with your kids—and then let it go; don't get all bitter and twisted about it later. At the same time, sort out the things that you aren't prepared to give up, and make arrangements accordingly. Sometimes, it's actually possible to combine activities that will please everyone if you give it a little thought; but more often, you'll have to arrange for the kids to do something else while you enjoy your favorite pastime.

If their mother hasn't taken the opportunity to disappear while the kids are with you (and she doesn't live far away in the first place), you may well reverse the usual visiting schedule so she relieves you by taking the kids part of the time, thus affording you the chance to do what you want. Incidentally, don't make a stink about it if your former wife wants to get away by herself at these times—you may be asking the same of her sometime. Other relatives like grandparents or uncles and aunts may actually want to have a piece of the action, if you can believe that. And your woman friend might be kind enough to take them off your hands to give you an hour or two.

If your children have friends in your neighborhood they'll spend a lot of time hanging out together, and if you're lucky, the friends' parents may also keep an eye on your kids as well as their own—but don't forget to return the favor. It may even be possible to take your kids to visit their friends who live closer to their mother's. It could be worth the trip because kids like to stay overnight. If you can work something out with the friends' parents, you might find yourself with a free night to yourself.

We might also mention that community agencies like the YMCA and the department of parks and recreation sponsor various recreational programs for children each summer, giving parents a chance to breathe while their kids have a good time. So you may want to obtain schedules of their summer services and activities. Some of their adult and family programs may appeal to you as well.

Considering even this partial list of resources that are available to help you look after them you may feel a little more confident about having your children for the holidays. Remember, all we've been talking about for the most part are the special *problems*. There are very special advantages as well.

These occasions may be the only times when things feel "normal" to you with the kids, when you have enough undisturbed time together really to unwind and have fun. It may also be the best opportunity you'll have to do some fathering—to teach them things you haven't had time for before, to get to know and encourage their unique talents and accomplishments, and to help them understand things they need to know, like your separation or divorce and how you feel about them. It's a good time for loving.

# 5. Parting Thoughts

In sharing our own awkward development as fathers, and those of our friends, clients, and others, our goal has been to encourage people like ourselves—men in the process of recovering from separation and divorce—to reawaken to the children they may have left behind, and to recommit themselves to the responsibilities and rewards of being fathers. We know how difficult each of these steps can be.

The shock, grief, and anger generated by the end of a marriage is in itself a considerable thing for people to overcome. For the separated father there is the added jolt of awakening to the realization that a family and children have been lost as well.

The resulting anguish and the catastrophizing about these things that often accompanies it combine to make it extraordinarily difficult for many men to see that they may not have to "lose" their children. But the possibility of actively continuing to be a father is obscured, not only by heightened feelings, but also by the consistent programming of our culture that has led men to believe that they are basically unnecessary to their children. In this way, the separated father comes to regard himself as an expendable, throwaway parent; he has no idea that he might be important to his children except perhaps as a provider, and when his marriage breaks up it may never occur to him that his children still *need* him.

He's further discouraged by the fact that he usually hasn't learned to take care of kids (or himself for that matter), often because he thinks these skills are a woman's province rather than a man's.

Others join him in discriminating against himself. Most of the people to whom he may turn for counseling, emotionally and legally, and who actually make crucial decisions about him and about his family, all tend to be in the dark about the importance of fathers;

they are bound by the same stereotypic notions about men and children as he.

Consequently, as a separated father you will probably have to struggle through a morass of ignorance and prejudice, yours and other people's, with only your own feelings about your children to guide you—if you are to emerge with some sense of importance to your kids, and if you are to explore the possibilities for recovering your role as your children's father.

Throughout your struggles to understand these things, as a disenfranchised father, you will likely have to cope with the emotional stresses of seeing your children for brief moments under disheartening conditions. You will probably be simultaneously engaged in a crash program to learn the rudiments of child care and housekeeping. And, in spite of all the horrors of separation and divorce from her, you may be shocked to discover the incredible amount of contact that will be required with your former wife because she's the children's mother, however awkward it may be for both of you. Childless couples can walk away from each other, but people with kids have to find some way of working co-operatively with each other despite their difficulties.

If you've found a new companion you will also have all of the problems of trying to balance the relationships between your woman friend and your children, not to mention the challenges of your own new beginnings with your companion. You may also have to deal with other important relationships that are in trouble because of separation or because of your attempts to recover your role with your children—such as parents and friends in the first instance, and your occupational and social commitments in the second.

Yet, while the jumble of feelings and the confusion about where you're going and what you're going to do may make recognition and recovery of your role as a father difficult, a recommitment to your children and a resolve to do whatever you must to re-establish yourself as their father can actually speed your recovery from the shock of separation.

Having meaning and purpose again in your life will offset the sense of defeat and depression that often accompanies separation and divorce, as well as reducing a tendency to catastrophize about "losing" your kids or remorse about "abandoning" them. Opening yourself to a new kind of relationship with your kids may permit you to discover your children as people perhaps for the first time, and yourself as a genuinely responsible and caring person.

Liberated from your previous one-dimensional role as a husband and "provider" you may take pride in your newly earned status as a parent and in your brand-new skills as a "houseperson"—feeling more responsible and self-reliant than ever before.

Paradoxically, you may owe much of this increased freedom from dependence upon women to women, some of whom may have taught you how to cook, how to run a house, and how to care for children. Indeed, in most cases the children's mother will deserve credit for pulling her share of the load, giving you the opportunity to learn your job as a parent. Though you may not realize it, you will also owe a debt to women's fight for recognition as people and first-class citizens, because their pioneering work has done much to set the stage for your fight to be recognized as a *first-class parent*.

Thus, in the process of separating yourself from a marriage and learning to be a single parent to your children—with all the experiences of being a "mother," and a housekeeper as well as a "father" which this entails—you may begin to move away from stereotyped ways of seeing and relating to women and toward recognition and respect for women as people like yourself. One consequence of this is that you may find yourself a potentially better companion in a new relationship, more prepared to enjoy a genuinely equal partnership with another person.

Perhaps the biggest winners of all will be your children. While they may tend to feel less bound by marriage contracts than we as a result of their experiences with us, they may also learn much broader roles for themselves, transcending the sexual stereotypes we learned, and allowing them to combine work and children with ease, or to be nurturant and loving as well as industrious and assertive. They may be better partners to their companions, without having to question the need to share things, and thus they may establish more fundamentally stable and satisfying relationships than we, based on mutuality rather than privilege. And we earnestly hope they may learn from witnessing our development as parents how to be good fathers and mothers to their own children.

We are grateful that throughout this arduous and rewarding process we have had each other to talk to. And we hope that you will be fortunate enough or wise enough to find other separated fathers like yourselves to share your experiences and knowledge with, and with whom you can find the validation and support you may need in being a father. There are many of us in the world now, at various stages in the process of becoming; we shouldn't be too hard to find.

# Index